Keeping His
Pants On

Until He Gets Home

Keeping His
Pants On

Until He Gets Home

For Women of All Ages

in Marriages of All Stages

Joyce S. Oglesby

ACW PRESS
Nashville, TN 37222

Keeping His Pants On: Until He Gets Home
Copyright ©2007 Joyce S. Oglesby
All rights reserved

Packaged by ACW Press
PO Box 110390
Nashville, TN 37222
www.acwpress.com

The views expressed or implied in this work do not necessarily reflect those
of ACW Press. Ultimate design, content, and editorial accuracy of this work
is the responsibility of the author(s).

Publisher's Cataloging-in-Publication Data
(Provided by Cassidy Cataloguing Services, Inc.)

Oglesby, Joyce S.

    Keeping his pants on : until he gets home / Joyce S. Oglesby. -- 1st
    ed. -- Nashville, TN : ACW Press, 2008.

        p. ; cm.
        ISBN: 978-1934668-00-9
        "For women of all ages in marriages of all stages."
        Includes bibliography.

        1. Sex in marriage. 2. Married women--Conduct of life.
    3. Marriage--Psychological aspects. 4. Sex instruction. I. Title.

HQ536 .O36 2008
306.8/723--dc22   0804

Printed in the United States of America.

Dedication

To Webby, an answer to my childhood prayer; a man of great patience and understanding, unfailing love and unparalleled support; a wise man for recognizing the value of my independence, yet appreciating my search for his wisdom and guidance in many situations. All who know him love him, but none more than I do.

Contents

Acknowledgements

We hold no match to God's perfect plan, His masterful orchestration of this thing some call fate, others destiny, or providence. His absolute ideal arrangement for this book, and many others to come, is a riveting testimony of relinquishing your dreams to the Creator of splendor. He has equipped other willing vessels to touch those of us with lofty ideas and promote us to claim the power from within. Years ago, He fashioned within Dr. Dennis Hensley ("Doc") the desire for greatness, and Doc rose to meet the challenge.

I liken Doc to God's "Paul" in this phenomenal arena of the sculpting of idiom. He writes with inherent mastery, speaks with commanding authority, and he laughs, lives and loves with a passion borne only from the heart of a true servant of God. His contagious thirst for achievement launches one to uncover the capacity to excel. His will serve as an interminable legacy. Not only are his words of wisdom preserved for now and generations to come, but products of immeasurable talent have achieved recognition through his skillful techniques of writing. Woven with his unwavering words of encouragement, these protégés continue to amass insight, humor, and enjoyment for millions of readers.

I am fulfilling a lifelong passion—that of helping others through writing. I surrender to a blessed emotion when

I pause to consider the privilege to study and benefit from sitting at the feet of the "master" —Dr. Dennis Hensley.

I extend gratitude to my family and friends who offered persistent prayer and support during this arduous task. I appreciate the labors of Faye Evitts, my strong critic, faithful fan, and friend. I feel especially blessed to have the friendship of Mansen and Deborah Way who have believed in, encouraged and supported my ministry.

1.
Having Sex for a Lifetime of Love

Prayer of the Modern Woman

Before I lay me down to sleep,
I pray for a man, who's not a creep,
One who's handsome, smart and strong,
One who loves to listen long,
One who thinks before he speaks,
One who'll call, not wait for weeks.
I pray he's gainfully employed,
When I spend his cash, won't be annoyed.
Pulls out my chair and opens my door,
Massages my back and begs to do more.
Oh! Send me a man who'll make love to my mind,
Knows what to answer to "How big is my behind?"

I pray that this man will love me to no end,
And always be my very best friend.

Prayer of the Modern Man

I pray for a deaf-mute nymphomaniac with huge boobs
Who is a good cook and owns a bass boat.
This doesn't rhyme, and I don't give a flip.
-Author unknown-

"I now pronounce you husband and wife. Now, sir, if you'd step over to the right and drop your pants, the nurse will administer your vaccination, then you may kiss your bride." Bam! Immunized. It's as simple as that. Never will he become fevered with temptation. Never will she fall victim to betrayal by the lure of the species of unfaithfulness.

In an ideal world, everyone would live happily ever after. All brides would love to have that security for their marriage. Sadly, many couples believe the nuptial vows inoculate their union, and they never have to worry about the maladies of matrimony.

I am not selling a spa or a YMCA membership to get you in shape and keep those home fires burning. I am not a dewy-eyed bride with visions of rapture designed to motivate you for temporary pleasure. Rather, I have been the wife of a minister for more than 35 years, am a mother and a grandmother, and have been a court reporter/business owner for 30 years. I completely understand the demands of being a career person while balancing the ongoing needs at home, and I offer a formula for a marriage destined to last a lifetime.

I didn't come by my life of love without bumps and bruises. During my childhood I had no example of how a husband and wife should love each other. My father was incessantly unfaithful to my mother. He was an alcoholic.

His violent nature did not subside when he drank. My mother and each of us eight children would suffer during his fits of anger for many years.

To be sure, I had no reason ever to want to trust a man in any manner. I was marked early in life. Having been introduced to sexual abuse at a tender age, I could have easily fallen into the pit with countless other women and grown to disdain men and everything they stood for. It would have been effortless for me to have become a part of the statistics of women who never attach emotionally with their men because of haunting ghosts. Emotional detachment brought on by a painful past can manifest itself in different venues. An aversion to sex would not be unexpected.

Women who tell me about their sexual abuse as a child oftentimes find themselves tormented in some manner or another in their adult sensuality. Many find it necessary to seek approval from any man and are never choosey. Consequently, they grow up absent of self-worth, entangled with multiple partners, and in and out of unhappy relationships and marriages.

Some abused victims fall in love, marry for life, and deprive themselves and their husbands of fully experiencing the abundance of intimacy because of either a fear or guilt complex from childhood experiences. These women never conquer the demons associated with such acts of perversion and, sadly, hold their husbands hostage in their silent prison. It never seems to compute that what happened to them was not their husbands' fault. They didn't hurt these women. All they want to do is love them, but these wives' inhibitions block their attempts.

Like myself, there are those who overcome and learn to accept love and to give it back. We also learn to forgive, which in large part is the first step to overcoming. Once forgiveness has been extended, moving beyond the past is essential in structuring a healthy, enjoyable sex life with the man you love.

My childhood experience offered me insight about the kind of marriage I definitely wanted to avoid. I knew early in life there must be more to love than what I had witnessed. So, I began to pray for God to send someone to teach me how to love. He answered my prayer. He sent me a wonderful teacher in the form of my husband. I also allowed myself to return love. It became a natural part of me to show my gratitude for the way he loved me, and these expressions of love have been mutually exchanged.

You may have been reared in a family free of abuse and infidelity. Your mother and father may have been committed to their marriage for the long haul. You could have experienced a delightful childhood, fallen in love, and expected to marry a man just like dear ol' dad. Your marriage is possibly the fairy-tale you always dreamed it would be. Or, perhaps it once was, and you find yourself wondering when everything got off course.

In my professional world as a court reporter, I have sat through more than 2500 depositions and court proceedings where couples have engaged in civil war, leaving behind shattered dreams, wrecked emotions, devastated finances, and broken and confused hearts of innocent children. Sharing in the ministry with my husband, there have been hundreds of accounts of couples mourning their marital breakdowns. Regardless of the courtroom or the church, in most cases, the husbands get the blame. Infidelity and/or pornography have been the perpetrators in a majority of these troubled marriages.

I am going to show you, however, that many relationships could have been spared the invasion of hardship had couples worked to protect and explore their intimacy. Marriage is a partnership designed to meet the needs of both parties. Intimacy is a need that never subsides in a healthy marital relationship, at least one designed to last a lifetime. The need for sex is something that should be regularly addressed for the benefit of you and your husband. Studies continue to validate that sex is good for a healthy emotional and physical well-being. It promotes a proper balance in your body.

This book simply offers easy, practical and attainable tips proven to reestablish and enrich intimacy in marriages. Some of the information contained herein will come as no great revelation to you. It is good for us to be reminded of simple reality. A woman's best intentions can get waylaid. Before she realizes it, months, perhaps even years have passed since she has made an effort to display her truest affection for her husband. The suggestions herein can be incorporated into a daily routine for every woman who desires to keep his pants on until he gets home.

NO GREATER PRIORITY

There is no greater priority for a couple than preserving the intimacy of marriage. I find the practice of that preservation to be pleasurable and fulfilling at many levels. I believe pleasure was exactly what God had in mind when He stroked the genius of reproduction. This idea of two shall become one was not just in the uniting of flesh in order to produce one flesh, to be fruitful and multiply. This procreation concept could have been

> *There is no greater priority for a couple than preserving the intimacy of marriage.*

through any form He contrived. He chose the spirit of intercourse as a means to accomplish His gift of life through reproduction. God also knew there would be women who would be barren. I know several who have struggled with this. Nonetheless, they have the ability to enjoy making love. He knew our sexuality would bring us pleasure. He knew it would bring union, depth of love, a longing for each other, and a desire to please.

As women, we sometimes send confusing signals to our husbands implying that we don't enjoy the physical act of sex. Or, maybe husbands are not confused at all. It could be the precise message they're being sent. This confusion can play a major role in the lack of interest of both parties in the bedroom.

I converse with few women who actually enjoy the act of sexual intercourse. It is alarming the numbers of them who abhor it. When safeguarded, nurtured and explored, many women find sex to be an extraordinarily pleasurable event. There must be good cause, however, for the countless women who don't enjoy this aspect of marriage.

If you are one of these women, it could be that you have never or seldom experienced an orgasm. If so, it is no wonder you don't enjoy sex. I would compare the absence of orgasm to having prepared an elegant gourmet meal followed by a heavenly dessert, yet never having tasted a single bite. It would be difficult to stand in the kitchen and slave over something that I would never get to savor!

Being unable to achieve orgasm can stem from a variety of medical as well as psychological issues. It may also be because your partner is not adequately striving to help you achieve orgasm. Could it possibly be that you have never communicated with him how to get you there? I would hope that your husband is the caliber of man who aspires to help you meet this need. If so, he will be receptive to your suggestions on how to bring you to climactic pleasure. You must, however, communicate your wishes and suggestions to him. It is the difference between the sexual act being a dutiful chore or that of an exquisite experience.

As we explore avenues to enhance your marriage, it will be beneficial for you to bear in mind the concept of which we all are keenly aware: men and women are uniquely different. I'm sure that comes as no great surprise. This design was an integral part of God's plan to compensate for each other's weaknesses and to draw on each other's strengths. We are not equal; however, we are neither inferior to the man, nor are we superior to him. There can be a workable partnership when couples are willing to honor God through the institution of marriage as outlined in His effective plan.

Your marriage should reflect your relationship with Christ...and most often does. The more intimate relationship a couple enjoys with God, the greater the understanding of love, honor and respect between the two. Devotion to each other becomes a natural part of the daily routine, and serving and meeting each other's needs rate high on the priority list.

I urge you to continue reading so that you will gain a full understanding of the message each chapter conveys. Every premise in this book has merit. If you apply even one concept to your marriage, it will improve your relationship both in the bedroom and out. Apply others and you'll witness greater improvement. Apply them all and you will begin to enjoy the full fruits of marital bliss.

2.
Fight for Those You Love

I don't care what you say about me, but you'd best not say anything derogatory about my husband or my children.

I, as most women, live and die by this philosophy. There are few women I know who don't stand ready to rip the heart out of anyone who attacks the ones they love. It's one thing for her to put them down, but don't *you* even think about it. If you cross that line, the fur will fly, and you stand to lose a friend for life. That's what we do – we fight for those we love.

MARITAL WARFARE

Whether you realize it or not, you are in marital warfare. You may be blessed with the most wonderful spouse. You may feel your marriage is soundly secure and unshakable. You may even believe that nothing or no one will ever come between the love that you and your husband share. You are probably very aware, however, that temptation lurks every day. It does not always come in the form of fleshly seductions, such as infidelity or pornography. Temptation takes on varying disguises. It may present itself through gambling, alcohol, drugs, and even apathy or depression. It can even adopt a disguise of emotional attachment of a co-worker, friend, or on Internet chat lines.

I recently consoled a 35-year-old friend whose husband decided they had become too *disengaged* to attend a marriage encounter weekend. He felt it would simply be a waste of time. The casualness of his statement led to much more serious conversation and, ultimately, their separation. When questioned, John was uncertain of whether he even loved Brenda any longer. He was willing to stay in the marriage for the sake of the kids but could give Brenda no hope for the restoration of his love for her. He had become caught in a slowly diminishing desire for her, and was uncertain if there were any romantic feelings left. She was stunned and distraught at what she was hearing. The evening was a disaster, as she bolted from the home to give him time to contemplate his revealing news.

Their marriage had been a struggle at best. The two were extremely different individuals. Brenda has always been very outgoing and very dramatic. John is more a loner and rather reserved. She is a controller; he is happy to relinquish. Suddenly, three children and fifteen years of marriage no longer was a high priority in his life. He was tired, bored, confused, and numb. He proclaimed there was no one else. She was bewildered, dejected, devastated, and lost. She feared for the emotional stability of her children, because at this juncture she was unwilling to live in a home devoid of love.

Brenda sat crying and mystified as she questioned her marriage. She realized John had not been himself for quite some time. Convinced she had tried everything she could to make him happy during the past two years, she was out of options. She recognized John was changing, becoming more withdrawn, very silent, less motivated, and seldom in need of her affection. I listened for hours as she berated her husband. She recounted his many faults, emphasizing his weaknesses. My heart ached for her as she spilled recitations of disappointments throughout their years of marriage. My heart broke for her as she seemed clueless about the battles she had going on inside her heart and mind. John failed to function at the same pace and manner she would have preferred, so Brenda had taken over his duties and responsibilities in order to accomplish her means. She was exhausted from carrying the burden of leadership in the home, as well as working nine to five and keeping kids and home in order. She had assumed the role of John's mother, and the lover in her had gotten misplaced in the shuffle of life.

She brushed back the tears as she asserted her physical appearance had everything to do with the diminishing of his sexual desire for her. "When he married me, I was cute. I had a knock-out figure. I was tanned and beautiful. Look at me now. Why have I let myself go? He kept telling me it didn't matter, that he loved me the way I was. He swore there was no one else, and I believed him. I think he's just confused because he thinks he has to be passionately in love to be in love. We're not passionate. Life gets in the way. What are we going to do? How am I going to tell the kids? This is going to destroy them. I'm uncertain exactly how I feel, but I'm pretty sure I'm done at this point. I can't do this anymore. I just can't."

"You don't have a choice, Brenda," I retorted. "You have to stay in this marriage. You have to fight for those you love.

That's what women do. You and John created a family. You committed to God you would love each other forever, until death do you part. No other couple in the world has done what you and John have."

She cut me off. She was quite puzzled, doubtful that I had heard a word she had uttered. "Joyce, we haven't done anything right. What do we have to show for our marriage? It stinks. It absolutely stinks. It's in shambles. He can't even tell me he loves me, and I can't live that way. I left him tonight. It's over."

"Brenda, no one could generate what you and John have during your years of marriage. The two of you fashioned love from chemistry. From that chemistry you produced lives that depend on you for their security and stability. No other two people in the world could have created Chris, Jordan, and Meghan. Your children are flesh of your flesh. They are your responsibility. You owe it to them to keep the family intact. You owe it to God to keep your covenant relationship together. You owe it to yourselves to continue the history you began. You can't just throw in the towel without a fight. It's just not what women do. We fight for our men and children, and you will fight for yours. You have not lost this war. You have *weapons of mass production* at your fingertips. You simply have to use them.

You have weapons of mass production at your fingertips.

"I've heard you run on endlessly about the things that make you crazy about John. Now, tell me what you love about him."

Brenda paused. She calmly and passionately began to paint a picture of John's strengths and virtues. It was clear that her love for him was not dead. She was overlooking the qualities she admired most about him. When she had finished, I told her, "John sounds like a man anyone could fall in love with." She began to weep.

"Now, begin by fixing what you know is wrong, what you really have control over, and commit everything else to prayer, time, communication, and patience. This unraveling of your marriage didn't happen overnight, and you can't mend it overnight. It will take time. But, you must be committed to the cause."

Brenda didn't quit. With further coaching, she opened her eyes to the ill seeds she had planted in her life. She began burying issues that had plagued her for years, putting the past far behind her. She examined areas in her life and began to pluck out what was bearing bad fruit. She put on her armor, picked up her sword, and she began fighting the battles one by one. She wrestled with her demons of control, her exclusion of John in decisions, her sharp tongue, her nagging, her motherly behavior toward him, and a myriad other issues brought to light in their heart-to-heart discussions.

John professed she treated him as though he didn't exist. He was, however, amenable to discussing their troubling issues. In doing so, he became keenly aware of areas where he had failed Brenda. She needed him to assume his role as leader in the home. He agreed he had backed away from those responsibilities. For the sake of the children, he chose to remain in the home, even though they *separated* for a while.

Both John and Brenda had felt sexually deprived. Their marriage had become busy, their love stale and boring. They realized their friendship had been lost along the way. Yet, the couple wasn't willing to walk away from a commitment to each other and to God. They began working through misunderstandings, recapturing their friendship, and reconnecting their passion. Brenda also worked hard at becoming more secure with her physical appearance. John confessed that although it never bothered him she had gained excessive weight, he was thrilled she had taken the initiative to begin a weight-loss program because of the instant boost in her self-esteem.

LUCKY INDEED

Brenda and John were fortunate in that they had remained faithful to each other and to God during this lifeless season in their marriage. Either one could have easily turned to someone else for comfort and companionship. Either could have sought someone else to meet his or her intimate needs. They could have found someone who would have given the affection and attention that is necessary for a healthy relationship. This couple was lucky some other lonely individual didn't approach one of them. A lonesome single co-worker hungry for attention makes for an attentive listener. An acquaintance who senses discontentment could make improper advances. Both were prime targets to be scooped up by an act of infidelity.

As I helped this couple work through their situation, I encouraged them to make a conscious decision daily to remain committed to each other. They are continuing to work through their *boredom* in their marriage. Life for them was not uneventful; it was always challenging with schedules. It was the bandit of monotony that took them by surprise and almost altered five precious lives forever.

> *It was the bandit of monotony that took them by surprise... Your family history is at stake, and you must decide that walking away is not an option.*

Brenda reported recently that their marriage had never been stronger. In all their years of marriage, John had never sent flowers on Valentine's Day. The roses accompanied what would become a prized possession for Brenda.

The card spoke of John's endless love for her, the pride he now has for his beautiful wife, and his reassurance that he will be there forever. This became a happy ending for a marriage that was headed straight to hell in a hand basket. Each of them made a conscious decision not to throw in the towel merely because their marriage had become stagnant. It was certainly tempting, and seemingly the easiest thing to do at the time. Their commitment to God, to each other and their children held fast with great rewards.

BLENDING OF LOVE

No one is immune to turbulence in marriage. Each day can present its own set of difficulties, trials, and temptations. These times will present themselves in your marriage; you can count on that. I know of none who has escaped the woes of some sort of turbulence. You *must* have a plan in mind to overcome the difficulties, to work through the trials, and resist the temptations. Your choice to stay committed to your husband strengthens your heart and mind to deal with the unforeseen obstacles.

You and your husband are one flesh. You are a blend of love, and from that you have produced a history. Whether you and your husband have children, plan to have children, or children for whatever reason are not a part of your marriage, your commitment to happiness and contentment affects many people around you. Every experience you encounter within your marriage adds to the uniqueness of your personal melodrama. The footage you run during the course of your marriage will be interspersed with a kaleidoscope of memories.

None of us likes to recall the hard times, but upon reflection we soon realize that those days are the very ones that provide us with depth and resolve. Choose to draw from the good that has been derived from a particularly sour part of your history. Hanging onto occurrences that bring bitterness and resentment is sure to suck the life out of any relationship. Preserving the pleasing history the two of you have created is critical in keeping the mood of love in the home, especially the bedroom.

UNIQUE HISTORIES

Let me tell you about my family history. My husband and I are diverse personalities. He has a quiet, diplomatic spirit about him. I am more vocal. I am fairly straightforward and highly opinionated. We both are lovers of life and possess high-energy qualities. We simply go about things in different ways. But we are one flesh. It is interesting that people often describe us as being two peas in a pod or cut from the same mold. Being different as night and day in many respects, we find it refreshing that we appear as a harmonious blend of personalities yet still maintain our distinctive characteristics. I have weaknesses, as does he. My strengths compensate for his. Webby's strengths complement my limitations. Together we work as great partners. It doesn't lessen our individuality, however, as we effectively serve in our varied occupations.

We have produced two children who possess some of our same qualities. They are very similar in nature. They even resemble in appearance. Yet they are each unique. No one else in this world could have created these two girls – only Webby and myself. Out of that, we have our marital history. It is a part of us that we are committed to continue to carve through the course of time. We now enjoy the products of their marriages to two fine young men. Oh, my gracious, what greater joy than that of loving grandchildren. I dare say nothing else compares. And each time we come together as a family unit, we expand the pages of our history.

I will fight for this history. It is inherent in me to do so. I pray you, too, will go to the front lines for the man and children you love. You must never choose to walk away from the commitment you have held so dear. Be careful not to allow disharmony to invade, much less set up camp in your home. Address issues that cause distance between you and your husband. Once you identify problems, you will be better equipped to find a solution before too much time and detachment come to pass. Your family history is at stake, and you must decide that walking away is not an option. Nor should simply "existing" in the marriage to keep family intact be an option for you. Make your marriage one that is full of loving, passionate experiences. Adopting an atmosphere of genuine intimacy between you and your husband is a perfect place to start.

Now, Fight for Your Passion

Your keen desire to strengthen your intimacy within your marriage demonstrates your willingness to fight for the man you love. I recommend that you begin to set goals for your marriage. Keeping him sexually fulfilled is a significant beginning. When you begin to explore your sexual horizons, you both will begin to enjoy a more satisfied home environment. You will walk into your bedroom at night and close the door on all the troubles of the world. When you open the door the next day, you both will be ready to face the world and all its challenges with contented hearts, resting in the knowledge that you are an invincible team.

3.
Commitment

No one falls in love by choice, it is by chance. No one stays in love by chance, it is by work. And no one falls out of love by chance, it is by choice.

AUTHOR UNKNOWN

Beth came home early from work one night much to Todd's surprise, and chagrin. Todd was sitting at the computer visiting a porn site. Beth had suspected this behavior for some time, but had never been able to prove conclusively her fears. Feeling betrayed, she sought advice. After listening to her bemoaning and dissatisfaction with Todd's actions, I queried Beth at great length about the level of intimacy the two of them shared. They were a young couple, not quite ten years into their marriage, and the problem would surely escalate if not readily addressed. She confessed the passion had waned during the last couple of years, but was due in large part to the fact she was rarely satisfied.

"Todd doesn't seem interested in satisfying my needs. He's content to get his needs met and then go to sleep. I just don't enjoy sex, so it's hard to get motivated."

I introduced several of the tips outlined in this book to Beth. She incorporated them into her marriage, and truly she believed it was what ultimately saved their marriage. Beth realized she and Todd both had work to do in the area of their sexuality.

Communicating to each other their needs for sexual fulfillment, they began to unravel the potentially love-gone-sour relationship they were headed toward. Todd was an elder and Bible school teacher in his church. He held a lofty position within the community and had a lucrative career. His addiction to pornography could have compromised every area of his life, and Beth and their children would have suffered at his loss as well. They were both willing to stand by the commitment they had made to honor God in the preservation of their marriage. Beth was willing to meet Todd's needs and to communicate as to how he could better satisfy hers.

Laura wasn't as fortunate in her marital dilemma. The thrill she and Adam had once known began to slip away long before they were willing to admit there was trouble. Laura had discovered multitudes of porn sites Adam had engaged. Eventually, the visual affair was no longer satisfactory, and Adam became physically involved with another woman. When Laura and Adam confronted their problem, he was beyond agreeing to work it out. At Laura's insistence, however, they came to talk with my husband and me. We sat for hours dissecting the issues and raking through the leaves of despair that had covered the couple. Webby (my husband) and I saw the situation for what it was. Try as we may, convincing Adam to carry through his commitment to his wife and children seemed hopeless.

Adam's jaw was set. "I'm moving on. She doesn't even make an attempt to meet my physical needs. She's so busy with the kids, it's as though I'm only there to bring home the paycheck. We're too busy to connect, to talk, to listen, to care. We don't even look into each other's eyes. I've just fallen out of love with her."

Laura countered, "I have nothing left at the end of the day. It's all I can do to work, run taxi for our children, keep house, and cook dinner while I'm helping the kids get their homework. I'm spent by the time we go to bed. But, I love you, Adam. I promise I'll do better. We can go for counseling. We need to work this out for the kids' sake."

"I'm sorry, Laura. The kids will adjust. They'll be fine. I want a divorce. I've found someone who understands my needs, and I'm much happier. Life is too short to settle for what we've become."

There would be no reconciliation for Adam and Laura. Their situation was confronted too late in the game. Adam was unwilling to resolve their mediocre lifestyle. He had already found stability in another relationship, and his marital vows to Laura were no longer a priority in his life. Laura was completely wrapped up in her routine responsibilities and totally unaware Adam needed more intimacy in their marriage. My husband and I were unable to convince Adam to reconsider. He was willing to disrupt the lives of his wife and three children and completely disregard his commitment to "love, honor and cherish till death do us part."

Countless scenarios such as the Adam-and-Laura saga have made their way to the divorce courts. In the ministry, our experience has been that the two most common and powerful dividing forces within a marriage are money and sex. Some people are willing to compromise all sorts of principles to attain them. When one party allows either of these forces to become a problem within the marriage, commitment to the partnership fades into obscurity and becomes secondary to selfish endeavors.

LACK OF COMMITMENT

What's the real problem with Christians and our lack of commitment today? Why can't we make a union between a man and a woman joined in the holy state of matrimony a workable scenario?

Lack of commitment is prevalent in every facet of life and has been for some time. We have become a disposable society. It is much easier to acquire something new rather than invest the time, energy and effort to fix what may be damaged. This mentality has permeated our marital relationships, and, thus, the family unit is in serious trouble.

We have witnessed this decline for several decades and have only begun to experience the consequences. Parents who are not committed to one another oftentimes come up empty in commitment to their children.

We have become a disposable society.

Future generations will struggle to formulate any definition of true commitment in relationships. What a vicious lifestyle we are coming to accept as *the norm* in our society.

Blended and single-parent families are issues at the forefront of every avenue we pursue. Our schools are besieged with unruly children who have no structured home life, no form of authority, no sense of respect, and no model for responsibility or commitment.

Churches today are faced with the dilemma of unmasking the deep-seated problems of marital relationships and how best to teach people to embrace the degree of commitment our grandparents lived by. Although their generation had its share of dysfunctional and troubled families, the evidence supports the facts they had fewer divorces, fewer STDs, fewer abortions, less drug addiction and use, and fewer blended families. While it is true our pre-baby-boomer grandparents sometimes married at much younger ages than is the norm today, we cannot ignore the level of commitment they maintained.

As wives, how do we secure the commitment that was promised to us by our husbands on our wedding day? How can we ensure that he will keep his pants on until he gets home? Let's get more personal. Where is your level of commitment as a soulmate to your husband? Does he have reasons to anticipate coming home to you after leaving work? Will he find solace and comfort in your arms when he gets home?

Some world is waiting to push his release button. Make it be your world.

Have you prepared not only the kids with anticipation of his arrival, but yourself as well? Will you rise to the level of meeting his needs when he walks through the door after being bombarded with demands and stress at work? What resting place will he set his sights on tonight? Will he be afforded the luxury of releasing his frustrations and escaping into a refuge of devotion and surrender, or will he again be left to seek that release through some other means? As he attempts to unwind from the day's injustices, some world is waiting to push his release button. Make it be your world.

UNMASKING PROBLEMS IN MARITAL RELATIONSHIPS

There has been a rising trend toward nude beaches, people walking the streets in their underwear, thong jeans, casual nudity on our movie, television and computer screens, and sex clubs. I contend this behavior is not a *natural* part of our thinking. From the moment sin entered the picture, modesty became a part of our conscience and at the pinnacle of our forethought. That single act of disobedience by our ancestors bore a seed of sin so great that it occupies mankind's entire thought process.

We are a sensual society, and sex a commercial commodity. Today, it is rare to see advertisements where a provocative and/or scantily-clad woman is not the sales promoter. By the time the commercial is over, you wonder what product it was they were selling. Most television programs are shoving cleavage, midriffs, and lots of thigh our way. Pornography has become a multi-billion-dollar industry, and much of it involves God's precious young children. The child sex slave trade is the fastest-growing black market, second only to drugs. It is at a demand level so great that we will continue to see the rise in abductions, sex crimes and murders among innocent youthful victims.

Yet another aspect of this poignant scenario is that pornography has invaded many Christian homes today. It has reached such an epidemic proportion that our churches must now address "porn and the Christian man" at weekend seminars. The Internet plays a tremendous part in the infiltration process. We must all accept our share of the responsibility for this dilemma – both men and women. Pornography, provocative commercials, and television and movie screens all project an image that leaves little room for competition by the spouse. Husbands partaking in this activity set themselves up for disappointment, disillusionment and, many times, divorce.

Today, we are more aware than ever of sexual disorders. There is a fine line between *insatiable desire* and *addiction* to sex. This is not a new phenomenon; it has simply been identified and labeled. Regardless of how it is labeled, each of us must accept responsibility to exercise self-control and rein-in our feelings without acting upon these lustful desires. Unfortunately, there will always be individuals who will succumb to the unquenchable desires that seem to escalate this addiction process. In most cases, this type of behavior must be addressed by a counselor in order to redirect the thought process of the addiction. I am more concerned with the prevention and/or intervention of such behavior in marriages. Our husbands' desire for sex is our responsibility as wives to fulfill; it is their responsibility to exercise self-control.

SEX, A KEY INGREDIENT

How do we get back to the days when the family unit was woven tightly and our children could count on mom and dad being there at the end of the day? I will not dwell on the myriad issues surrounding this topic; however, I will focus on what I believe is a key ingredient to a successful marriage: SEX. This common denominator puts us all on a level playing field and is a factor that could possibly secure a long-term commitment on the part of our spouse.

Our husbands' desire for sex is our responsibility as wives to fulfill; it is their responsibility to exercise self-control.

We are aware there are many dimensions to a successful marriage, but we cannot possibly downplay the importance of sex in a healthy marital relationship. It is a crucial component in the structure of our relationship as husband and wife, and one that cannot be dismissed as a casual or passing season in our lives.

Sex may seem an unlikely topic for a minister's wife to teach, but ministers have sex, too. (I know this comes as a shock to some, but it's true.) And guess what? We enjoy it. It is my keen desire that if you long for sexual fulfillment in your marriage, you will embrace the information contained in this book with an open and challenged mind, a spirit of adventure and spontaneity, and a heart desirous of preserving the precious gift of marriage to which you and your spouse are committed.

Years of experience in *counseling* women who have been broken-hearted over situations of infidelity on the part of their husbands have inspired me to share what I consider to be valuable insight into the needs of a man. I use the term *counseling* loosely, because *I am not a counselor* by profession. I have, however, been exposed to countless incidents of women, and men for that matter, who have found themselves in a marriage that has become one of boredom, insecurity, involving people who are questioning their love and devotion for a spouse, and even those who have crossed the line and breached their vow of faithfulness.

It is interesting, whether in the legal or clergy setting, most instances of marital conflict and discontentment that have evolved into infidelity can trace the root of the problem to the lack of sexual intimacy on a fulfilling level between the couple. While I don't have the luxury in my career to explore the innumerable circumstances surrounding irreconcilable differences, I have interrogated those who seek advice on a more personal level in our ministry. As delicate a subject as it is for people to explore problems and concerns about someone else's marriage, the reservation exhibited in examining intimacy issues speaks a thousand words as to why so many marriages fail. Many people are too reserved to probe deeply enough into the issue of marital intimacy and evoke the true heart of the problem at hand.

We find ourselves embarrassed to broach the subject of sex with our spouses. We shy away from exploration of our erogenous zones. Timidity about our likes and dislikes with regard to sensuality sets us up for a calculatedly boring bed. Many women not only shy away from talking about sex, they dismiss the thought of it being a problem at all. Women are sometimes too eager to cast blame for their suffering sex lives on the mundane tasks of the day, such as rearing young children, taking care of finances, the interference of in-laws, or pursuing careers. Under closer examination, we might find much of the dilemma stems from our lack of interest and response in the bedroom.

WIRED DIFFERENTLY

Our society is well aware of the Women-Are-From-Venus-Men-Are-From-Mars concept. It is no revelation that God made us different. He formed Eve from Adam's side; Adam saw Eve, and they were naked and felt no shame. Eve ate of the forbidden fruit; they *realized* they were naked. They were comfortable with each other's nakedness until they sinned; then modesty became an added factor in their relationship.

God even assigned different tasks to the man and the woman at the very beginning. The man was given the task of caretaker of the garden, keeper of all, namer of the animals and worker of the land. Eve was to bear children and be a helpmate. Her given responsibilities were very distinct right from the outset.

Our God of infinite wisdom designed man to desire woman. It is no mistake that your husband has sexual needs and desires you. Women possess an innate desire to please a man. This desire is defined by our need for security, commitment and to be nurtured by our husbands. This combination has served to fulfill God's plan for procreation. You can be confident, however, He did not intend for the act of reproducing to be all work and no play.

Examine the Song of Solomon. Its message is erotic. It

communicates longings and desires for the flesh that are sure to stir even slumbering cravings. Read this song of romance and substitute yourself and your husband as the lovers. It is an all-consuming passion that will sweep over your heart and cause you to welcome everything about him. This sacred performance – the art of love – should be one enjoyed by the husband and the wife, as designed by God, and should serve to enhance, enrich, and inspire a marriage.

ONE PLUS ONE EQUALS ONE

As you can readily appreciate, I strongly believe intercourse should be reserved for the sanctity of marriage between a man and a woman, as intended by our Maker. The institution of marriage is the purest form of true harmony in a relationship and spares a couple multitudes of problems in varying forms, whether it is six months or sixty years into their relationship. Allowing

There can be no expiration date for commitment in our marriage.

promiscuousness outside the confines of the covenant of marriage serves only to present itself with possible physical and/or emotional problems that must be dealt with in marriage.

That said, commitment to one spouse is still very much a process. It should be engrained into our thinking by committed parents, and become a heritage we continuously strive to maintain. The value of preserving commitment for THE one equals one marriage for life. There can be no expiration date for commitment in our marriage. It is a virtue that spills over into all areas of marriage and serves to heighten a couple's sexual pleasure.

You have made a pledge to one man. No longer can you

dwell on how Bart or Jim or Larry floated your boat! You can't close your eyes and imagine how Tom kissed you so perfectly, Martin knew exactly how to touch you, Richard knew your every thought, Jeff your every need. None of us should forget how devastating the comparison issue could be to both parties.

On countless occasions I have heard women, whether in marital despair or simply sharing their emptiness, compare their husband's performance to that of a past lover. Why this act of lovemaking comes so natural to some men and not to others is as much a quandary as why the great majority of them seem to love blondes. Comparing your man to someone in another chapter of your life will only serve to lessen your promise of a life-long commitment. Each time I hear a wife reminisce of days gone by with other men, it is a riveting reminder of why the plan God set out for the institution of marriage still remains unprecedented in its approach. One man plus one woman equals no comparisons!

BE COMMITTED TO FULFILLING

One of the saddest injustices in marriage can be the lack of fulfillment and satisfaction in the bedroom. In addressing issues with couples who are having marital difficulty, I have found one partner will almost always acknowledge he or she simply is not satisfied sexually by their mate. The union of husband and wife should be one of closest intimacy, hearts at their fullest, with trust and security sealed, so that neither should have cause for concern of breach of their promises to one another.

Commitment has its rewards. I have personally found it easy to meet my husband's sexual desires because our commitment to each other is in place. It is equally important for him to meet mine. Meeting one another's needs sexually was a commitment we made to each other very early in our marriage. We discovered at the outset that communication in this area would be essential in bringing about complete satisfaction for both of us.

If you are lacking sexual fulfillment, chances are someone is not committed to doing his/her part, and someone is certainly not telling the other what he/she needs. The art of making love involves much detail. The element, brought to the bed by you, of being devoted to pleasing him will ensure you of a heightened sexual experience. Taking care to set the tone for love befriends your attitude of commitment, and we'll discuss these aspects in other chapters. These details are your companions in the art of love. Real sexual pleasure takes an effort of creativity and a tearing down of walls, but the end result is rewarding. I don't mind having *just sex* every now and then, but on a scale of one to ten, I rate *lovemaking* to be an experience like no other and one that brings a marriage to its fullest cycle of completion.

ALL MEN ARE NOT EQUAL

Please allow me to make this one disclaimer. All men will not respond to the formula in this book for a terrific marriage. So, please, if this does not work for you, *do not* feel as though you have failed. I grew up in a very male chauvinistic and patriarchal home. An abusive father and six brothers could have caused me to become quite disillusioned about men in general. My mother would have never measured up to my father's expectations, nor would he have ever been satisfied with her performance in any area. He was never happy with himself; therefore, his restlessness caused everyone associated with him much unhappiness as well.

All men will not respond to the formula.

There are many men just like my father; they are drastically unhappy with themselves, no matter how wonderful the woman is who loves them. There are men who are lacking in bedroom manner; those who are control freaks, male chauvinists, domineering, afraid to love, unable to talk, devoid of tenderness, lacking in self-control. And then, there are just your run-of-the-mill sexual perverts, if you will, and one woman would never be able to satisfy their needs. These men are committed only to themselves. They lack the ingredients necessary for any woman to be able to please them.

If these types of issues are at play in your marriage, I would urge you not to feel you are a failure. I would implore you to seek counseling for yourself and your spouse to work through these obstacles. Many men will not act upon the request for counseling, but some do, and I have seen it turn a marriage around. If your husband is not amenable to seeking joint counseling with you, I would encourage you to go alone and explore possible remedies for your individual situation.

I could exhaust pages on what God meant in His plea for us never to be unequally yoked. Lack of communication in marriage is just one of the many issues that can surface. Many times, however, even God-fearing men have trouble communicating properly in a marriage, but almost always the one who has no need for God generally makes no concerted effort to begin to understand how to love his wife as Christ loved the Church. When unequally-yoked couples try to blend these marked differences and make a palatable situation for all, they are usually setting themselves up for a huge disappointment. One party's expectations are going to be unmet, if not both.

If you are among the many unfortunate women who have a husband who is cold, and at his very best impossible to reason with, my best suggestion for you is to commit him to prayer and to try the formula outlined in this book anyway. You may be pleasantly surprised at what God can do for you through your intimacy with your mate. He enables you to open doors and eliminate walls that may have been barricades for years. Aspire to make your man's heart soft. It may take you more time than you feel you have patience and energy for, but it is definitely worth the investment. He is the man you committed to spend your earthly life with, so he is your gift to open. Don't ever give up as long as he is within the scriptural boundaries of the marital covenant.

COMMITMENT IS FOR KEEPS

Commitment to your marriage is *for keeps*. I love sitting in the audience when my husband performs a marriage ceremony. His service is not your usual do-you-take-this-bride perfunctory event. He personalizes each ceremony and makes the couple feel the commitment being made is like none other that has ever been made, and he's right. He draws them into the understanding of Paul's instruction about love. "Love is patient, love is kind. It does not envy, it does not boast, it is not proud. It is not rude, it is not self-seeking, it is not easily angered, it keeps no record of wrongs. Love does not delight in evil but rejoices with the truth. It always protects, always trusts, always hopes, always perseveres. Love never fails." (I Cor. 13:4-8 NIV)

Webby goes on to explain how all-encompassing this act of love is to the two who are about to become one flesh. Before the bride and groom pronounce their vows, a vivid picture has been painted for them as to the lifetime bond they are sealing.

Naturally, the enamored couple seals the vows. I have yet to see anyone decide *nah, that's not for me.* Of the hundreds of ceremonies I have witnessed, every couple has marched out with the trademark grin on their faces, having pledged to love, honor and cherish the other till death do they part. Commitment is an absolute with them . . . until trouble in paradise knocks.

Once trouble is on the prowl, what then happens to integrity? What about the promise before God and the hundreds of witnesses? What happens to the working out of difficulties? Thousands of couples who make this same sort of pledge each year are joining the walk-away society we have come to know. Commitment then becomes something meant for someone else's marriage, not theirs. It becomes an old-fashioned way of living. It becomes obsolete. The expiration date is up, and we toss it away like expired milk.

Commitment is a thread that must be rewoven into the fabric of our family units. While it is incumbent upon both parties in a marriage to feel this urgency for commitment, as women we must step forward and do our special part in preserving this vital quality in our marriages.

Commitment is a daily decision you will make. I wake up every day deciding that I am committed to my husband. It is a conscious decision. It is a necessary decision. It is protection for our marriage as I go out into my little world. It is a buffer in

Thousands of couples are joining the walk-away society we have come to know.

the face of temptation that will surely come my way if I'm not careful. Satan would love nothing more than to see a Christian family fall. He delights in such victories.

Because I guard myself through prayer and a steadfast decision to stay committed to our marriage, I am ready for the pitfalls life sends our way. Life happens. It happens to all of us, regardless of our calling. Life has its share of trials. It can test our patience and make even the best of marriages a little rocky at times. When commitment has been decided on a daily basis, it narrows the options of how you handle situations. There is no turn-tail running or walking away from those you have promised to love a lifetime.

The ideal scenario is for you and your husband to make this daily commitment together. Creatively produce ways in which you can recite the forever-do-us-part vow on a romantic evening you two share. Over candlelight dinner is a good place to start. Perhaps when you lie beside each other after a great love-making session is a time to reinforce the promise. Make the commitment in front of your children. Go ahead, tell each other how much you love the other. Kiss passionately in front of your kids. Throw your arms around each other and hold that pose for a lingering time. Let them roll their eyes, cover their head, make some groaning complaint of how cheesy you are. Regardless of their adverse reaction, it is reassuring and protecting for your children to know you're in this thing for keeps. It is a fortifying and bonding ritual that allows them to focus on worries of their world and not mom and dad's woes. Children face enough struggles without having to be concerned if their parents are going to survive the marriage.

Renew your vows so that your children can hear your commitment to each other. Don't be concerned with how *silly* you, your husband or family may feel the first time you do this. It will become more natural as you make it a routine part of your family life. It doesn't need to be something you do out of habit, although an anniversary date is as good a time as any. Or, just pick a date out of thin air for a more congealing statement. The renewal needs to be a very special time. It should be a memory-making moment you share as a family.

For small children, having one of them be the preacher, one a maid of honor, flower girl, or best man can really be a fun time for them. Even your teenage kids can enjoy being silly with you during this time. Bring some laughter and levity to the affair, and they'll get drawn right in. There'll come a time when it is totally uncool, but they will enjoy it and tell you they did someday down the road. Teaching your children about commitment is possibly the single most important tool you could equip them with for life. Showing them how committed you are to your love for each other prepares them for their lifetime relationship with a mate.

COMMIT TO INTIMACY

Remember, commitment as a couple is a two-way street. Women often fall into the trap of placing the brunt of the responsibility for commitment on the man. It is just as necessary for you to assume your place in this partnership you have accepted. It is not enough to ensure that you prepare his favorite foods, keep the house clean and in order, adopt a positive atmosphere within the home, and understand the necessity of giving him time to watch or play sports, tinker with his cars, or embrace some other hobby. You must be ever mindful of the urgency of meeting his sexual needs as well.

For you, your daily commitment to him will energize your desire to meet his needs – physically, emotionally and sexually. Keeping him happy and content at home ensures that he takes his pants off for no one but you.

4.
Attitude

A minister decided to do something a little different one Sunday morning. He said, "Today in church, I am going to say a single word and you are going to help me preach. Whatever single word I say, I want you to sing whatever hymn comes to your mind."

The pastor shouted out, "CROSS." Immediately the congregation started singing in unison, "The Old Rugged Cross."

The pastor shouted out, "GRACE." The congregation began to sing "Amazing Grace, how sweet the sound."

The pastor said, "POWER." The congregation sang, "There's power in the blood."

The pastor said, "SEX." The congregation fell into total silence. Everyone was in shock. They all nervously began to look around at each other, afraid to say anything.

Then all of a sudden, from way in the back of the church,

a little 87-year-old grandmother stood up and began to sing, "Precious Memories, how they linger."
AUTHOR UNKNOWN

For many years, the "S" word was unspoken by a mother and/or father to their children. It was the absolute blush word. I can recall my father pecking my mother on the cheek only one time in all the years I was home. I witnessed firsthand no signs of affection, embracing, or fondling, and my mother certainly never shared with me the talk about *the birds and the bees.* My first exposure to verbal communication about sex was the sex education film that was shown each year to the entire fifth grade in school, and it was lacking at best.

Those of us in my generation and before were much more sheltered about sex. Whatever we weren't told, we drew our own conclusions about. One could only surmise that since it wasn't talked about openly, it had to be something very dirty; and if it was dirty, it couldn't be fun. It certainly was something every male wanted, and it didn't take the female gender long to discover that.

Every generation has its share of promiscuous girls who are willing to *put out* on a regular basis. Sadly, we are plagued with more of those girls at an even younger age today. No longer is the word *sex* one that is kept silent in front of our young children. Sex is flashed across every screen on major networks as people hop in and out of bed with anyone and everyone – single, married, divorced, young, old, and everything in between. Sex is hammered into the heads of our young people through the music they listen to, through chat rooms and My Space online, and their peers. It is introduced to them at extremely young ages in school in forms of safe and/or oral sex, even experimental sex, as our administrators pass out condoms. In the event they miss something with all the information available to them, believe me, there is sure to be an acquaintance in their lives who will know all about the topic and be more than eager to share his or her knowledge without the benefit of our input as parents.

This is a travesty for many of our young girls and boys. They have been taught no standard for preservation of their bodies for the one special person they are sure to want to marry someday. The majority of our children will enter marriage with a set of problems that could potentially materialize into monumental entanglements in their relationship with their spouse. A disturbing trend among today's Christian parents is not only to condone, but to give their blessing on live-in relationships of their young adults. It comes as no surprise, naturally, when we witness many Christian adults making that same choice themselves.

It is incumbent upon us as parents to give our world of children a healthy, educated and godly message about sexuality. We need to protect them from the pitfalls of reality that will come from giving up their purity before marriage. Abstinence and commitment are two ingredients that need to be reintroduced into our culture. They are protection for not only their physical health, but for their down-the-road happiness and fulfillment, as well.

As distressing as it was years ago having a limited and skewed impression of sex as being something *dirty*, to the extreme, it is worrisome that our children are far more knowledgeable than they should be at tender ages. This knowledge shapes attitudes toward sex. Everything from inhibitions to exhibitions has taken its toll on our marriages. People have an awfully lot to battle when they enter a relationship with less than healthy attitudes of sex. It is the parents' responsibility to impress upon their children that it's not okay to sleep together or live together before marriage. It is outside of God's will for their lives. It's outside of His plan for the entity of marriage. There are far more risks involved today than years ago in promiscuous sex, but the purity of the flesh being compromised can certainly muddle the mix in the best of marriages.

SEX IS A MINDSET

Despite this *openness* of sex today, many women find themselves absolutely unfulfilled in the bedroom because of the stigma attached to sex - *doing it* is something she must do to gain approval from a male. If she gives him what he wants, she's sure to win his heart and acceptance. This pervasive attitude among our women, young and older, that they must perform in order to get the attention they crave can often serve to spoil the sweetness of love-making in the marital relationship. Feelings such as this must be redirected so as to adjust thoughts and attitudes with regard to sex if we are ever to experience intimate sexual pleasure with our lifetime mates.

Sex begins with a mindset, especially for women. The physical allure it holds for men is where women feel we were a little short-changed. Women much prefer to be drawn into the sexual act emotionally before we engage in the physical performance. Your husband may not recall the sarcasm in his comments this morning when he later approaches you for sex at night, but you may still be stewing over his distasteful words. You may have had a horrendous day with work or kids or friends, but his day may have been filled with less commotion. He is ready for action; you are ready to crash. The two of you may have shared a relaxing evening, but your thoughts are far from an intimate encounter. He has not shown any signs of affection or tenderness throughout the day, yet he immediately approaches you for sex at bedtime. You may feel a

Sex begins with a mindset, especially for women.

sense of devotion but no sense of sexual desire for your husband, because he has failed to meet your needs time and time again. You may even be convinced he is only after self-satisfaction and cares nothing for your enjoyment or sexual pleasure.

How do you readjust your thinking from a complete turn-off for whatever the reason to a *baby-I'm-yours* attitude? Is it possible to consciously turn your state of mind into a positive reaction to his approach for sex? The answer is irrefutably yes.

It has been my experience that mind over matter and the power of positive thinking are beneficial tools in accomplishing any task at hand. There is power and wonderful rewards in the spirit of acting your way into a better way of thinking. Your mind can be cluttered with many issues. This clutter will crowd out energy you could invest into redirecting your thoughts related to making love. It will be important for you to rid yourself of mundane daily issues that can exhaust and distract you from focusing your attention on him. It is equally important that you divest yourself of stored-up painful historical events between you. Recalling them from time to time and cashing in the ticket to squabble serve only to cause resentment, hostility and dissension.

Until you can rid yourself of feelings that hold your passion at bay, you may never enjoy the sweetness you knew when you were newlyweds. It is time to let the past go. And remember: the sun sets on a new past every day. Revisiting his wrongdoings serves only to rob you of the harmony you desire for your marriage.

FORGIVEN? FORGET IT!

Initially, I would encourage you to release any resentment, animosity, or ill-will you may be harboring toward your husband for some transgression against you, however big or small the infraction may be. For instance, infidelity is an egregious act of betrayal, yet many couples decide to work through the numerous issues that arise when one party has had an affair. My advice to many wives, as they seem to be the ones who have the most difficult time of letting go, has been that should you decide to make the marriage work, you must *never* bring it up again. When you proclaim that you will forgive, you must decide to bridle your tongue with respect to what has happened in the past. While it is noble and dutiful to try to work through a situation of infidelity, it is not fair to either party to live in a miserable existence for the sake of keeping the marriage intact. Holding on to hurt serves no purpose and profoundly stalemates a healthy relationship. Likewise, holding onto mistakes you may have brought upon yourself can be equally as damaging to your relationship with your husband. It is the past; unlock the shackles.

Larry and Maggie were the perfect couple. They worked hard to attain their material possessions. They loved each other, had a beautiful child, and began to establish investments for early retirement so they could travel and see the world. Then Larry was unfaithful, and their world began to unravel. Neither one wanted to dissolve the marriage. He was sorry; she was willing to see it through. However, they have never been able to reestablish the relationship they once knew. Maggie is bent with anger and resentment, and she continues to remind Larry of his irresponsibility. She has tormented him for years and has managed to bring great suffering to both parties. Larry is now an alcoholic, and when he can no longer take her ranting and raving, he leaves. They separate for weeks on end, only to find themselves back together trying to start all over. Neither one wants to say good-bye, but Maggie has never understood the benefits of casting aside the past and working toward a better future with Larry.

Stan and Rhonda shared an almost identical scenario. Rhonda, a more forgiving spirit, was able to bury the past offenses of Stan's and move forward in their marriage. In a private setting, Stan shared that Rhonda had never mentioned the incident again. He was grateful she was so forgiving. He related how he struggled with forgiving himself more than she seemed to struggle with forgiving him. He went on to reveal that his devotion was truly rich, and he was amazed at his wife's response to him. Applying the fundamentals set forth in this book, their outward affection for each other assures the world they live in that their relationship will be stronger than ever before.

Clare can't get past the hurt of Bret's unfaithfulness. "It was just one time, and he says it just caught him totally by surprise. He assured me it would never happen again, but I just can't get it out of my head." Tears were streaming down her face as she recalled the account of her broken heart. "I just don't know how to get back to where we were."

Forgiveness is truly an important factor in developing a healthy attitude in a marital relationship. It is the very foundation of our Christian principles. When you offer forgiveness, you wipe the slate clean, and it is as though it never occurred. Draw from the history you

Begin to work on a new history that will repair your shaken foundation.

have made with your husband that is pleasing to recall. If you have had cause to forgive injuries in your relationship but have a difficult time forgetting, highlight it and delete it from your hard drive! Begin to work on a new history that will repair your shaken foundation. We must remember, in order to enjoy a full measure of forgiveness from Christ, we must practice it to the same degree.

Many of the women who have discussed this forgiveness

issue with me have confessed, after much probing, they feel perhaps they hold on to an injury in a relationship as a form of punishment, especially when the act has involved infidelity. My question is always the same: "Punishment for whom, him or you?"

Punishment? Are we sixth-graders or adults? In any situation where forgiveness has been an obstacle in moving forward in a relationship, the penalty for the wrongdoing is always more severe for the person who holds onto the wrong, whether it be the perpetrator or the victim. Much of the time what occurs is a situation where the victim, in an effort to bring about restitution for a wrong, punishes not only herself/himself, but everyone else in the family as well. The party who lays claim to the misgiving will be the impediment to the restoration of the marriage.

Sadly, many women never exhaust the subject of infidelity.

Almost every man who has spoken to me of an affair he has gotten caught up in has shared that one ingredient is necessary in repairing the marriage: his spouse must get beyond forgiveness. Many of these men struggle year after year to *make up* for the wrong they have done, but their wives hold them hostage. She doesn't really want to talk about it since, after all, she's forgiven him. She merely wants to keep throwing the darts at his heart. While she may or may not have forgiven him, she certainly hasn't forgiven herself for the role she played in it. He would rather not discuss it at all. In fact, his preference would be to pretend it never happened and to pick up with their lives and live. These men confess, however, that if she could talk it all out of her system and be done, they would be happy to sit and endure the agony, just knowing it would be behind them. Sadly, many women never exhaust the subject of infidelity.

Prayerfully, you have a relationship that is open to communication and you both share your feelings freely. If you have worked through a situation like infidelity and moved on, let it go. Lesser offenses deem forgiveness, also. How foolish we will feel when we come to the end of a journey, whether a marriage or life, only to find we hurt ourselves more by holding on to grievances. Forgiveness is for you as much as the offender, regardless of the transgression. Only through forgiveness will you be able to purge your mind and heart of hurt and/or anger and appropriately shape your attitude for giving and receiving intimacy that will satisfy both of your physical needs. Softening your heart through forgiveness allows you to concentrate on other areas of your attitude that are important in attaining intimate pleasure.

TOO TIRED FOR SEX?

On many occasions, I am completely exhausted after a day's labors. As a mother of two, now with grandchildren, a career person with a household to run, errands and sports to keep up with, a minister's wife's duties to fulfill. . . the days' responsibilities never seem to end. I'm fully aware of the times my husband is in need of our intimate contact. Some days I feel completely depleted of any energy; yet, I realize I should muster up some reserve for vigorous activity, somehow. And, so, I do.

It is a matter of literally psyching myself up for a time of sheer unadulterated pleasure. I am amazed at the level of response my body kicks in when I allow my mind to receive it. I fall asleep completely exhausted, but with such gladness in my heart that I have willed myself

Forgiveness is for you as much as the offender, regardless of the transgression.

into the right way of thinking and brought pleasure to my husband, and received pleasure as well. Sex is a great avenue to release frustration.

What a bond we create. How we respond to each other the next day – such tenderness and playfulness and laughter. When we were young parents, it was good for our children to see us interact with each other in this manner. It was healthy and nurturing and made for a very happy home environment.

You, too, can overcome the sense of being too exhausted for him at day's end. You will be surprised how effective it will be. Take just five minutes to regroup your thoughts. Think of endearing times between the two of you. Tell yourself you need this as much as he does. Adjust your attitude. The results will be rewarding and beneficial.

REMEMBER WHEN

I have found such truth in the idiom "the more things change, the more they stay the same." This is especially true when it comes to the male species. We must understand *and* accept the fact that men respond to us in a physical manner. Now, please understand, there are exceptions to every rule, and certainly we cannot fit *all* men into this mold. There are men who can put their physical nature on hold and actually get into the emotional side of themselves as well, if not better, than women. Bet you dimes to donuts your man is not one of those, and he operates just like ninety-nine percent of all the other men in the world – physically.

When you stop to consider this, what better compliment could your man give you but to be turned on by your body? The desire . . . the spontaneous desire to touch you, to kiss you, to embrace you, to hold you, *to lay you down* is a *blessing* in your marriage, and your attitude should reflect such. His desire for you is an important ingredient in your sex life, and it secures a lifetime of commitment to each other.

When I feel a lack of sexual desire, whether it be lack of energy and not feeling like being intimate at all, or sometimes just wondering why I ever married him to start with, I find it beneficial to take myself back to a moment in time when I could have ripped his clothes off and eaten him alive. You can relate to that, can't you? For me, *a song remembers when*, and I'm instantly revisiting that moment in time: what he was wearing, his cologne, his hair, his breath, his touch, the passion – everything is new and refreshing once again.

I am reminded of how much deeper our love has grown, even with mishaps along the way. We all have them. It's no different in a minister's family than in any other family. There have been good times; there have been bad. We all need reaffirmation of our decision for our choice of mates, and the bumps along the way merely serve to enhance and deepen the relationship. That depth is what's left when the physical intimacy part of the relationship becomes difficult to keep up with.

Allow me to caution you that the bumps and bruises should never discolor the original hue of your relationship. The sense of thrill in the assurance that he's the only one who can *do it* for you is a part of your relationship that needs to be kept in motion and never allowed to stray. Maintenance in this area is important if you are to thrive as an intimate pair.

Make a list in rank and order of what you love most about your husband. Think back to what you were first attracted to, and fast forward to today. He has probably matured in a lot of areas, and I'm quite certain there are areas he may have lost ground. Place this list in a private place for you to refer to often. Perhaps with your makeup, your underwear drawer, on the inside of a cabinet door so that when you open it, you are reminded of his attributes you love most. This list will be a great motivator, and will serve as a sedative at times as well, to spur you on to *placin' a lovin' on your man.* These are the reasons you chose him as a lifetime mate. You certainly want the world to know you made a wise choice.

HE NEEDS SEX

You must never forget the one element in your husband's makeup that makes him tick when everything else is falling apart, and that is his physical need. You may be emotionally distraught and bent, and while he may join in with your emotions for a while, he automatically goes back to his physical capacity and becomes the man who must be loved by you. It is part of a man's makeup. Once men have talked about an issue, it's done, over, they're on to the next matter at hand, and that need for sexual fulfillment is waiting around the bend. And, trust me, if you don't do the job, there are ten million lonely women out there who will! They are on the prowl for innocent victims, and you may just as well deposit him on a platter, ripe for the carving.

GO AHEAD, FANTASIZE!

The act of making love is something that should be dwelled upon by you. "What, fantasize with my husband? Aren't fantasies played out with a hot, sexy celebrity or an imaginative knight in shining armor?" I am most certain every woman has gone there a time or two in her daydreaming. Reserve these for your husband. Yeah, that's right. Go ahead, try the fantasy with your husband. It's exhilarating. Be totally adventurous, out there and really stretch it. Then, fantasize about something attainable and make it come to fruition.

Forget about how silly it makes you feel. That's part of the fun. Remember: you act your way into a better attitude. So *what* if you don't have a husband who's into game-playing entertainment. He might think you're nuts at first, but just show him how powerful it makes you become in the bedroom and, believe me when I tell you this, he will be all about the fantasy from then on.

Realistically, this is not going to be a once-a-week, or perhaps even a once-a-year adventure in your life, and perish the thought, maybe only for the first few years of your marriage. I can recall several of these occurrences in a year's time at first, but that was BK – before kids. It just doesn't happen as often after that, and even less as age creeps up on you. But, never allow that spark in your relationship to die completely. Just as being young at heart keeps you more youthful as you age, it is equally important to keep that youthfulness in your marriage. Faster-than-life seasons will cover you like kudzu. These times can prevent you from submerging into your relationship with your spouse, but these little spicy *adventures* will keep you in sync with each other as the busy-ness of everyday life spirals around you.

It need not be elaborate or costly to execute your fantasies. For less than ten dollars, you can have a night worth remembering. I can recall many such occasions in our marriage, but perhaps one of the most memorable times was when my husband opened the garage only to find me completely naked save for the rolls of plastic wrap tightly encompassing my body and a big red bow atop my head. The sight would've made Marabel Morgan proud. (Thought he'd never get home after I called him that day. I sweated off a few pounds with that one!) The fun really began when he was trying to rip off the plastic wrap, and it was the truly clingy kind. Surprises such as this make great memories, and it preps your mind for more creative ideas ahead.

Getting in the mood can be creatively gearing up for an elaborate sexual encounter with your husband, or it can be as simple as psyching yourself up for a routine night of sex. The idea is to think your way into the mood for love. Turning your husband's idea of *getting sex* into *making love and having fun doing it* is pivotal to your attitude.

MORNING DELIGHT

Oh, and don't forget, men love sex in the morning! Why is that? Your body has had time during the sleeping hours to rejuvenate itself. Your skin becomes very supple and soft. They love to hold you and stroke your skin when it's fresh with the morning light. Make it a frequent start for your days. Just as you must plan to get up earlier for your devotions or some project you're working on, or to work before the household gets up and going, you must plan some time to wake yourself . . . and then him . . . and start your day off with some intimate time between you, even if it is brief. What a difference in your day when you start out with the bonding of love with your spouse. Talk about an attitude adjustment, this is a sure fix.

Think your way into the mood for love.

What will he have on his mind all day? Y-O-U. Certainly not some cute little thing down the hall at his workplace. This new way of thinking you are beginning to adopt is a little added insurance that no one else out there should be able to tempt him in an area that he might be craving otherwise. Morning delight whets his appetite for the day, and he's assured the main course and dessert is yet to come.

THE POWER OF SEX

Sex is an appetite, an insatiable desire men have. It is a powerful driving force in your man's life. We cannot escape that fact no matter how hard we try. For those of us who have been suppressed as a woman at some point in our lives, it can be a difficult pill to swallow. Though women have managed to rise like cream to the top in today's society, we are still reminded on a daily basis that this is a man's world.

Although men seem to abdicate leadership responsibilities within the home, it is women who seem to acquiesce to the idea. We pick up the ball and run with it, letting our men off the hook. We see many successful women highly capable of running companies, managing finances, children, home life, and even assuming the spiritual leadership within the family unit. I believe many mothers today are minimizing the importance of masculinity. Fathers assume minor roles in leading the family at present more than ever before.

Regardless of this independence (and calamity at times) women have managed to create for our gender, there remains in us the desire to be pleasing in a man's eyes. We can ignore the issue, put it on a back burner, pretend it doesn't exist, but the gnawing is there. And, guess what? It's as it should be. We were designed to desire man.

God created Adam in His own image; Eve followed to add completeness to man's life. There was a need in Adam's heart and soul almost immediately that nothing could fill like that of a woman. We revolve around our man. We were created to complete him. Much of what we do in our day is to please him, and most of us love nothing more.

By now, you are probably thinking we can't have it both ways – an independent woman and catering to a man at the same time. Yes, you can. I have been a career woman for almost 30 years, made many decisions on my own, set my own goals, worked at an incredible pace, juggled career and husband and children and church, not always in that order, and I still maintain that I love chivalry. It is not dead. . .yet.

I very much enjoy working in the professional world, and I can tell you I suit-up to meet that world realizing I deal mostly with men. I must gear my thinking to the way they think, my ideas to those they respond to, and my production at their speed and deadlines. For every woman out there running the show, there is some man looking on to see what she's capable of doing. Lest we forget, other women are watching also, and in complete honesty, this is another important facet of a woman's driving force.

In order to be completely successful in adjusting your attitude about your sexual relationship with your husband, stop playing the game of "women are the same as men." We are not. We are gloriously different in every respect. It doesn't mean that I am below him, answer to him, nor am I above him. It simply means . . . we're different. We share different responsibilities because of our physical makeup. I may be able to do many things that he does, and sometimes do it better, but there are some things I am glad I can beg off because I am a female. He is put together with unique qualities different from me. And I'm happy for that.

The sooner we accept this irrefutable fact, the sooner we will begin to relinquish our stubborn will that can keep us from enjoying every part of our relationship with our husband. I know you hate to hear this, but it is a man's world, cut and dried. I would hasten to add it would be a very dull world without the female. We add flavor and adhesiveness to everything about his world. I know of no hot-blooded man alive who would take issue with this.

Allow this thought to settle in your heart for a moment,

and then get back to the goal – that of preserving your intimacy with the man you have committed to love for a lifetime. The thought becomes less threatening, less controlling, and less demeaning. Recognizing and accepting your husband as the main-stay in your home, the provider (even though your salary may exceed his), and someone who deserves respect from everyone in the family unit will keep your heart in tune to love him.

Again, I realize not all men are deserving of these lofty positions in the home. I have seen women turn these situations around in their homes through adjusting their attitude about their husband. Reshaping his self-esteem through her positive attitude softened his heart, and the couple began enjoying the love that drew them together in the beginning. I would be remiss, however, if I didn't tell you I have seen men who were unaffected by any attempts their wives made to create a balancing and harmonic home life. It is frustrating, I understand. My advice is to pray and seek counsel.

So, What Changed?

Once you decide that you perhaps need to readjust your thinking about how to enhance your love life, you will want to recall some times when everything seemed to click. *What have I done in the past that really pleased him? Where was I emotionally at that time? Was this early in our relationship? Were there children on the scene then? How did I look then? Was my hair short; was it long; what color? Where was he in his career? Where was our health at that time as opposed to now?*

We must be in touch with factors that change over time. Many variables in a relationship can alter how we respond to one another at a given season in our lives. It is not so important that we address those verbally, although that would be ideal. What is important is we know in our hearts and minds how and why we've arrived where we are today.

Many men are incapable of talking through feelings or sharing frustrations and emotions with their wives. They feel it's a sign of weakness or maybe they just don't know how to verbalize their feelings, and so they harbor their thoughts and their wives are left trying to define what went wrong. This can lead to tremendous consequences later in the marriage.

If you have a spouse who fits this category, you can come to a great understanding of what's going on with him simply by being observant of the man you love. There are windows of his heart only you can look through. Use that insight to fit together the puzzle pieces of why things have come to the point they have in your marriage. As women, we are called to be many things in life, even a psychologist at times. We assume roles and responsibilities we don't always have proper training for, but we somehow manage to muddle our way through. Trying to get things back on track for our husbands and/or families can be tiring. It is a sacrifice on our parts, but that's what women do often and best for our families – we sacrifice.

LOSING *YOUR* SELF

There is one aspect that must be addressed in order to make any relationship ideal. You must understand it goes against the grain of everything pushed down our throats today. However, it is wisdom taught by our Lord centuries ago. It is insightful beyond measure when a person grasps the full extent of its power. What a conversion would transpire if the world could understand its significance. While you may not change the *whole* world in adopting this rule of thumb in your life, you can certainly make a difference in *your* world.

What is that key that unlocks avenues of harmony? *Losing the* self *out of* your! It's a simple concept, but perhaps the most difficult thing for our *me* society to grasp.

Pair yourself with any other individual. Think of your relationship with your husband, your daughter or son, your mother, father, siblings, your in-laws, friends, or co-workers. Now, contemplate the flavor of those relationships. Which ones are seasoned with harmony? If your answer is all of them, you can pat yourself on the back. You are most likely a salt-of-the-earth type of person. If some of your relationships are good and others a little distasteful, you need to examine those interactions and give yourself a true picture of any improvement you can afford. Sometimes it's the other person's mix that spoils the feeling. If your observation is that everyone you have teamed yourself with leaves a little sour taste in your mouth, I would hazard a guess your leaning is more to your selfish nature.

> *The key that unlocks avenues of harmony:* Losing the self out of your!

You may be pleasantly surprised how tranquil your life can become when you decide to lose the self from within. I'm not suggesting *you* don't count. That is far from the healthy approach to life and not what God intended for you. I am suggesting, however, when you have no expectations for receiving anything from people, you will find yourself being less disappointed.

Anytime you personalize a situation, or make it become more about you than the person you're dealing with, you lose focus of what you have set out to accomplish. If you can pinpoint what you want in your life, try giving it to him instead. You'll find yourself getting it back. In other words, if you want respect, give him respect; if you want forgiveness, give it to him; if you want love, give it first. Well, you get the idea. This principle works in the bedroom. Strike out to please him beyond his expectations. You'll soon have a man wanting to please you in the same manner.

In order to be a great lover, you must totally lose sight of yourself. You are in this act of love-making for one purpose and one purpose only: that of pleasing your mate. The pleasure for you will be there. It may not be immediate, but it is a process you are working through. You must share with him what your needs are as you go along. His response should kick in and become that of pleasing you as much as you please him.

By adopting this attitude, you begin to redirect a bumpy marriage. If your marriage is fixed but dull, you will reignite the spark of energy necessary to preserve your intimacy for years. You'll find frustration is diminished in many areas of your life, and giving of yourself becomes a joy. You then begin to experience blessings you would never have known had you been in the relationship for self. You do need to protect your physical and emotional health, and so I would never suggest subjecting yourself to abuse or misuse by others. Harmony in the home, however, is often found by those who keep self out of the picture.

As women, our days are filled with complexities and diverse demands. Between spouse and children, work, and home responsibilities, our days begin with our heads spinning with agendas for everybody else. We can get bogged down in detail-oriented schedules

Harmony in the home...keep self out of the picture.

and game plans, and when things don't quite stick to that agenda, we can quickly begin unraveling. We become too absorbed in our self-perpetuated itineraries and, unfortunately, our families suffer. By the end of the day, we're completely wrung out, overwhelmed by the thought of meeting one more demand and removing ourselves from the mix yet again in order to please one more person. Life comes at us at such a high rate of speed that we meet ourselves coming and going much of the time. We're women. We juggle time and thoughts and energy, and we find precious few moments to indulge in set-aside time for us. Once our day settles down, it's hard not to be selfish with what little time we manage to squeeze out. We need a moment.

Many times when I sit down at ten or eleven o'clock in the evening, my husband will glance over with that indisputable gleam in his eye and ask, "Ready for bed, Honey?" How natural it feels to snap back with, "Forget it tonight, Bubs!" When I am wise, I simply remind him this is the first opportunity all day that I've had to sit down and just relax. Give me just twenty minutes or so, and I'll be ready for action. I need those few minutes to regroup. He doesn't mind.

Men usually don't mind being put off if they are as understanding and loving as Christ intended. *Just come over and sit with me on the couch, or give me a good massage to my back and shoulders, rub my feet, bring me a cup of hot tea, just dote on me a second and watch the magic happen.* That's the ideal response I'm looking for. Sometimes he does give me that much needed attention. If he doesn't, his feelings don't subside, so I must adjust mine.

I know you want to, but don't close this book. Keep reading!

I can't allow myself to think thoughts such as, *I've been at life all day, running and making things happen for everybody else, I'm done for the day, I've had it, I'll give nothing else.* It's tempting, believe me, but I have to remove myself from the scenario. He is more important than I am at that moment. Many times, he realizes I'm worn out, and he passes for the night. We have both passionate history and compassionate understanding in our sex life.

IT'S OKAY TO SAY, NO

When Webby and I were engaged, an elderly friend of mine gave me a piece of advice. He told me if I would take a jar and drop a black-eyed pea (remember, I'm from the South) into the jar each time my husband and I made love the first year, by the end of the year, we would have enough black-eyed peas to cook a meal. But, he continued, the second year, take a pea out of the jar for every day you miss making love. You'll find the jar will empty quicker than you filled it!

My friend was wrong . . . at least about us. Perhaps I was bent on proving him wrong, but it became a challenge to keep that jar full of black-eyed peas. I didn't keep the jar of black-eyed peas for longer than two years, because the challenge was not a chore; it was a pleasure. Making love was a routine part of our marriage. It was something we both looked forward to, and we took advantage of every opportunity we had. Neither was crushed in spirit, however, when the other's agenda didn't incorporate sex in the day.

Abstinence in a sexual relationship is perfectly acceptable. My husband and I have found that abstaining from our sexual activity, whether by design or through unavoidable circumstances, makes the passion mount and the reunion sweeter. In fact, scripture supports a time when you should separate and spend a season of fasting and praying.

We have both passionate history and compassionate understanding in our sex life.

"The husband should fulfill his marital duty to his wife, and likewise the wife to her husband. The wife's body does not belong to her alone but also to her husband. In the same way, the husband's body does not belong to him alone but also to his wife. Do not deprive each other except by mutual consent and for a time, so that you may devote yourselves to prayer. Then come together again so that Satan will not tempt you because of your lack of self-control." (I Cor. 7:3-5 NIV)

Abstinence should be by mutual consent, as pointed out in this passage. Be careful not to withhold sex from your husband as some form of *punishment* for something in which you are in disagreement.

YOU ARE MORE IMPORTANT THAN I AM

My husband and I have based our entire marriage on the concept of *you are more important than I am.* This is the advice he has given to couples he has united in marriage. Through the years, we have shared this advice with couples having marital difficulties. When you keep the needs of everyone in the family at a higher regard than yours, everyone's needs are being met. . .all the time. It is a concept that works and makes for a happier home environment. You can't out-serve the other. The investment you make comes back with resounding rewards. It doesn't matter if it's in the home, the workplace, at church, or in social circles, it will always serve you well.

This motto *really* works in the bedroom. When you remove your expectations and your eagerness to be pleased, you lose yourself into what will completely satisfy his needs. When you satisfy those needs to their fullest potential, you will cash in on a great return. Suddenly, you find a man who wants to show off his virility, to perform beyond any expectations you could have set to begin with, and to take you places you could have never dreamed up in a million years. It becomes his ambition, his goal, and his strongest desire to please you in return. The only thoughts he'll entertain of dropping his pants will be how he'll perform for you once they're off. Satisfaction will be your just desserts.

His pleasure and happiness will become a part of your lifestyle, and it has been borne out of an attitude of *selflessness*. You will discover you have established a foundation that will withstand many storms. You will have created a bond temptation would be hard-pressed to sever. With all the forces we have working against us today, it is urgent we do everything within our power to fortify this sacred institution of marriage.

Again, I realize this concept is quite contrary to what the world teaches us today, but it is what God has told us for centuries – to lose ourselves. Paul admonishes us, "Do nothing out of selfish ambition or vain conceit, but in humility consider others better than yourselves." (Phi. 2:3 NIV)

> *When you become selfless, you become complete... in joy, in love, in self.*

Go ahead. Take your *self* out of the mix. That's right, don't think about number one. When you become selfless, you become complete: complete in joy, complete in love, complete in self. Sounds like an oxymoron, but it becomes blatantly apparent when you put it into practice.

IT MAY NOT BE YOU

Another word of caution for women who have selfish husbands: if you have gone to the table with a feast multiple times and have left hungry, *he* needs help. There may be a deep-seated problem over which you have no control. If you have given your best, your performance should never be underrated. It is important for you to keep a healthy self-esteem, one that would not damage you psychologically nor cause you to feel less than the woman God has created you to be. I would implore you to encourage him to communicate with you and talk about what the problem is, and then you and/or your husband pray about the situation.

5.
The Look

A woman marries a man expecting he will change, but he doesn't. A man marries a woman expecting that she won't change, and she does.

AUTHOR UNKNOWN

IT'S NOT SUBMISSION, IT'S LOVE

As I contemplate the text that will follow, I must begin with a disclaimer to the readers who may never get to know me on a personal level. I do this for fear you will leave with the idea I am *old-fashioned* in my thoughts, or I am *subject*, if you will, to my husband. I am very much a twenty-first century woman. I'm a business owner. I'm independent and come and go as I please. I keep him apprised of my schedule, which is far more hectic than his. He then knows what time to have dinner ready when I get home. He takes care of his laundry, I take care of mine, and at times, we take care of each other's. We have a tremendous understanding and respect for each other's careers, and we each routinely adjust our agendas to accommodate the other.

There has been a great deal of misunderstanding throughout the years over God's instruction about wives submitting to their husbands. The scriptures divide the responsibility of the husband and wife in a marital covenant. A man who *expects* his wife to submit to him completely ignores the passage of scripture that speaks directly to him about loving his wife as Christ loves the Church. Because my husband practices this in his love for me, I find it a pleasure to submit to his needs.

I AM WOMAN, AND I LOVE IT

I consider it an honor to be a woman. I love my femininity and all the frills and thrills accompanying it. God bestowed our gender with a high calling and placed us in an indispensable role. It is in the fabric of our very nature to aspire to be a helpmate for our husbands. I have confidence in knowing I would make it in this world alone; I am a survivor. Yet, a large part of me *enjoys* and *needs* attention from a man. The fine art of being a female in today's society is blending independence and femininity while making it workable for both ourselves and our mates.

> The fine art of being a female in today's society is blending independence and femininity while making it workable for both ourselves and our mates.

Women are truly blessed with the skill of multi-tasking. We go through life juggling schedules and adjusting our lives at every turn simply to accommodate our families' needs. It is what we do, and for the most part, we do it well. I often look back on a day and thank my Lord for giving me the energy to get done all that I managed to accomplish in that day. We are, by design, movers and shakers. Man may be labeled as the leader in the home, but most every woman would agree, she is the manager. The title in and of itself encompasses tremendous responsibilities, yet we routinely juggle, rearrange and strive to keep everyone happy in the process. It can be exhausting being a woman; but still, I wouldn't trade it for the world.

While the feminist movement brought about wonderful advantages for women, it also brought a set of added burdens. We no longer have *only* the responsibility of child-rearing and keeping up the home, we must also add a career into our schedule. We have become accustomed to the two-income cash flow in our family budgets. We are motivated to acquire material possessions. Setting aside the material blessings, the cost of living is so great that most women cannot afford the luxury of staying home to rear children. Parents who choose to be in the home during this time may be called to sacrifice in some areas. Single parents may be left with no choice but to work. It is simply where we are today as a society and the choices we make as individuals.

I enjoy the 21st century benefits afforded to women, but I must admit I miss chivalry. The art of courtship is dying. I believe men are confused about what their role should be in this regard. They're even afraid to compliment a woman when she looks good because some men, and women, have taken it too far and there have been consequences. I find it refreshing these days when a man opens the door for me; it happens less and less frequently. Although I am quite able to open my own doors, I love the courtesy of the favor extended to me as a woman when a true gentleman is on the scene.

GET LOOKED OVER, NOT OVERLOOKED

I love the sensation I get in looking my best for my husband. I love the challenge of turning his head, of *dolling-up* just for him and having him approach me and tell me how I turn him on. It is the driving force behind most women to be appealing to a man. To quote the late, great Mae West, "It's better to be looked over than overlooked."

We females have our own inimitable way of wrapping those men around our little fingers. Our first experience began with our fathers. What is it that pulls at those heart strings between a man and his daughter? It is a sweet sight to behold. I love watching feminine little girls. They priss around

> *It is natural that we respond to the opposite sex with both a spirit of capture and surrender.*

and play dress-up with high heels and boas. They doll up for school, fuss with their hair that has to be just so, they swipe on lip gloss and purse their lips just like mommy. They have an innate femininity. We are driven to impress the male gender. It is natural that we respond to the opposite sex with both a spirit of capture and surrender.

Regardless of how bad the economy may be, you rarely see it affect the business at beauty salons. We can usually find means within our budgets to afford cosmetics, perfumes, new clothes, shoes, purses and all the accessories to complete a certain look to which we aspire. The countless hours we spend in front of the mirror, as tiring as it becomes, renders a surge of confidence and expectation that empowers us to move into a highly competitive market – seeking favor from a man. I love being a woman.

Why waste time in front of that mirror if you don't do it right? Go ahead, *think* sexy. You truly have an exception-to-the-rule husband if he doesn't like the sexy look. I would hazard a guess that ninety-nine percent of breathing males enjoy a sexy woman. All men have different ideas of what *sexy* is to them, I understand. He's your husband; you find out what makes him respond, what his *sexy button* is.

Some women think they don't have a sexy bone in their body. If you *think* that, you're probably right. I believe sexiness, too, is a mindset. A large percentage of your ability to be sexy is empowered within your mind, not your body. Again, it is the power of positive thinking that can add dimension to your abilities in any given area.

I make a mental note when my husband responds to a certain color I wear. I wear it often, although it's not everything in my closet. He needs to see me in other colors to appreciate the one color that *gets him going*. I pay close attention to a particular style of clothing that may spark a compliment. I dress for him. The way I style my hair has always been more for him than for me. He loves long hair; I find it to be quite a chore. We have compromised over the years. He declares if I am happy with it, he will be, too. I strike a happy median in length, color and style suitable to us both, and he is pleased.

You can be sexy without being offensive, or immodest. You can be sexy without compromising your principles. You can be sexy without being immoral. It is a look you aspire to that is pleasing to your husband. It may be a suit. It may only be a pair of jeans and a tee-shirt. If he likes it, wear it. Remember: if your man is loving you as Christ loves the church, he will not

> *Some women think they don't have a sexy bone in their body. If you* think *that, you're probably right.*

expect you to dress in a provocative manner. Tell him you'll save that for the bedroom.

When I am ready to walk out the door to my job, I wait with anticipation for an approving compliment from my husband. He empowers me with confidence and an energy

I need to face the business world. I am a woman. It is important for me to present myself to everyone I encounter – men and women alike – in an appropriate manner. I believe I can look professional *and* appealing, and I work to achieve that end result.

Like everyone, I love lounging around in my PJ's when I don't have to go out and do the dress-up thing. But, I have to be really careful not to get in the habit of lounging around slovenly. It'll really rev his engine for you to dress for the occasion at bedtime. You can never go wrong with seductive. On the nights we anticipate a time for us, I make sure I pull out my *Victoria's Secret* apparel, or something else he especially likes. (Sometimes my birthday suit is all that's necessary to get the job done. To him, it's about as sexy as it gets.) It's a sure way to get the evening kicked off in a positive way.

What? You don't look good in those things? Oh, you don't feel sexy. Imagine that. Unless your husband is one of the men who has been tainted by pornography or the commercials flashed in front of his face day in and day out, he will think you look absolutely voluptuous. Trust me, a husband who truly knows how to love will look at his wife's body in a totally different light from the way she does. I know from personal experience. And remember: sexiness is a mindset. You think sexy; therefore, you are. And go ahead, turn off the lights and light a candle. My philosophy is some things look better in the dark!

My philosophy is some things look better in the dark!

Forget the flannels! Indulge in sexy lingerie. Pick out the color, the style, the charm that is uniquely you, and get several of them. Wear them often. An every-night event will lose its effect, so use your judgment as to when they come out of the drawer and onto your body. Just make sure you have a supply. Men love it.

I will pass on a secret few women understand the importance of. Get rid of the peach fuzz on your face. You know what I'm talking about; those little fuzzy hairs all over your face. Shave them! Yes, I said shave them off. Some women wax them away, or use electrolysis to remove the unwanted nuisance. Whatever method you desire is fine and your choice, but get rid of the fuzz. Years ago my dermatologist told me the secret of a man's youthful look. Everywhere they shave stays younger longer, and from observation, he was right on. Shaving your face removes the dead cells from your skin.

You will not need to shave every day as a man does. In fact, you will only need to do this once every four to six weeks. Unless you are a woman with a problem of heavy, dark hair on your arms and face or have a high testosterone level, you will not likely be subject to a face of whiskers. It will not grow back stubbly. If you are uncertain of how your face will respond, experiment on an area at your jaw line underneath your ear where it is not noticeable. It took me awhile to convince my daughters to do this, but they see its benefit now. A man would much rather stroke and kiss a smooth face than one tickly from the *fuzz*. You will notice a remarkable difference in the application of your makeup, and in the sunlight or moonlight, your face will have a radiant glow.

Your personal hygiene is extremely important in maintaining a sexy appeal. Stay well manicured and groomed, including your hair. Shower and be fresh for your sexual encounters. It is a respect the two of you should seek if you want a truly romantic setting. I am often surprised by the men and women who complain of the lack of appropriate hygiene on their spouse's part. It does make a difference in your sex appeal.

FIT FOR LOVE

I can't talk about fit for love and fail to broach the importance of keeping ourselves in shape. My husband and I recently conducted a marriage class where we had married couples ranging from the ages of twenty-three to eighty-three. We allowed the opportunity for the couples to submit questions the last three nights of the class – pink cards for female, blue for male. We had numerous questions from the male population about how to approach their wives delicately about taking pride in the way they look, how they could encourage their wives to exercise with them, to dress more attractively, and on and on.

It is easy to be lulled into the fallacy that once he's married, he'll love you any way you are. Once women bear children, most bodies are absolutely never the same. There are a few of those – God love 'em – who readily return to their hundred-pound slimness. Most women spread in the pelvic area, stretch in the abdominal area, and sag in the everywhere-else area! We pick up those extra few pounds during the pregnancy; we vow we will work until it comes off. Six months come and go, we're still fighting the extra weight. Only now, since we have much less time for ourselves than ever before, we have managed to tack on a few extra pounds, and now we're dealing with a ramped-up rump, super-sized thighs, and a bloated belly. Then, the next child comes along and. . .. Well, you get the picture.

What are we thinking? I know we took that vow seriously. You know the one – *for better or worse*. But if we are honest with ourselves, we don't like the way we look, so how can we expect him to?

I have witnessed countless women who have gotten divorced, and once they're over the shock, depression and anger, immediately hit the workout scene. It suddenly becomes important for them to get back into shape. After all, if they're ever going to be *marketable*, they must look their best. They develop buns of steel and six-pack abs and begin dressing more youthful and sexy (even provocative, unfortunately). Imagine how the course of events could have been altered had they taken on that same passion *before* he had found someone else.

Rhonda and Brent had been married for more than twenty years. Their children were out of high school, and they had become early grandparents. My husband had counseled with them on several occasions during the teenage years of their children. Their marriage was rocky at best. We feared their marriage might not withstand the storms. Rhonda had become so depressed that she had really let herself go. She was a beautiful lady, but her exterior had become harsh and dull. Brent was unhappy and restless, but he was a good and righteous man. He stood beside her, but confessed that their romantic love had really suffered.

After listening to the principles set forth in our marriage class, Rhonda and Brent tackled the issue of their dying romance. Brent had always been attentive to fitness, so Rhonda decided to make it a pursuit of hers as well. For an entire year, she accompanied Brent to the YMCA and began toning and dropping the pounds. She not only took off pounds, but she managed to take fifteen years off her age! It has been gratifying to see this couple's affection for each other take on a whole new meaning. They confess their marriage is stronger than ever, and they have a new appreciation for each other. They attribute their new-found romance is substantially due to Rhonda's efforts in reclaiming her femininity. Of course, they hasten to add that communicating and exploring each other's desires have opened up comfort zones they had never experienced before. Their friendship has grown, as well as their honoring of the Lord in their home life.

I realize there are physical conditions that hinder many

women from maintaining their pre-marital figure. I also am keenly aware how age can alter one's weight considerably, even after the age of twenty-one. It is obvious America has become an obese culture. The foods we eat, the processing our foods go through, the fast-paced convenient regimens we have allowed for ourselves have all taken their toll. We are obsessed with diet plans, primarily because we must be.

We have become very sedentary in our work and homes, and it is necessary to maintain a workout program of some sort for good health. Even our children's playtime has changed dramatically throughout the years. Unless children are actively involved in some sport, they get little exercise. It doesn't take much effort to push the buttons on the remote of the television, or the buttons of the video games and computers.

I recently battled the weight issue. Having joined ranks with menopause, doctors were content to dismiss my rapid, excessive weight-gain issue and extreme fatigue as being hormonal. I conceded for a brief while. After all, I'd never been in that place before. Having settled on a regimen of hormones and realizing these concerns were not going away, however, I took charge of my health. Weight and fatigue were simply not the norm for me, and it caused me to question the proper functioning of my thyroid gland. With much persistence and going through several medical professionals, I found an internist who was equally as concerned about my weight and exhaustion. He ran more blood tests and set me up for a series of scans for my thyroid. He discovered I had hypothyroidism and nodules on my thyroid gland.

My research propelled me into not accepting the standard it's-just-hormonal answer. Many women suffer with a thyroid condition that is casually dismissed by the medical profession. I would suggest to all my readers never to give up. Throw a temper tantrum if necessary, but get someone to hear you when it comes to your health. You only have one shot at living on this earth.

Individually, we should take charge of our health. But as important as good health is for us personally, we need to understand the importance of staying fit for our husbands. Naturally, we are more appealing in his eyes when we keep our bodies at their healthiest. We certainly feel more confident about how we look and how we present ourselves to him, and to others.

When you have the heart-to-heart sharing time about how best to meet his needs, don't be offended if he tells you he would like for you to lose a few pounds. Or, you could spare him the uncomfortable ordeal, and you the insult, by asking him if your losing weight would improve your sex life. I know when I keep my weight down, I feel sexier in those cute little nighties. When I feel sexy, my performance in bed increases dramatically.

All women who have had children will appreciate the bit of wisdom I am about to impart to you. Kegel! It is important we keep those vaginal muscles tight. This is the easiest exercise to do because you can do it in your chair at work, standing at the sink, driving your car, anywhere, anytime. Keeping those muscles tight adds much more pleasure to your sexual experience. (An added tip: it helps keep your bladder muscles in better condition, as well. You'll really appreciate this someday.)

Keeping yourself fit maintains your energy level. It helps shape not only your body but your attitude. You feel good about how you look, and you can't wait to show it off to your husband. If you do all you can to maintain the look that is appealing to your husband, you won't have to worry about where his pants land when they come off; they'll be at your feet!

6.
Prepare Your Bed

My husband came home with a tube of KY jelly and said, "This will make you happy tonight." He was right. When he went out of the bedroom, I squirted it all over the doorknobs. He couldn't get back in.

AUTHOR UNKNOWN

We have a rule at our house: Whoever is out of bed last makes the bed. When the occasion falls to me, I sometimes take extra time to *prepare my bed*. I have a fairly good idea what the day will entail, and that is my barometer for knowing if our schedule might allow a special night. Like most folks, however, we have learned you can never count on anything for a certainty and, as the course of events change during our days, we adjust our schedules accordingly.

Preparation of my bed entails simplistic tasks. Time permitting, I will change my sheets while he's in the shower. I love crawling in bed with him with a fresh change of sheets. I also simply pull the sheets back just a tad so the bed is really inviting. I have my bottle of aroma therapy setting on the nightstand ready to spray just before we get into bed that night. I pin a "Pillow Talk LoveNote™" where he lays his head, with our favorite chocolate mints beside it. I pull out a nightie and lay it across the bed. I want him to see it before he leaves knowing he'll carry the image in his mind all day, anticipating the night and daydreaming of other intimate moments we have shared. I lay the groundwork for the night ahead.

LIFE HAPPENS

Sometimes the night comes off as planned, sometimes it doesn't. We are human. Life happens. It doesn't always work out, but in case it does, I'm ready. After a long day's work, I change into something more comfortable, and I am reminded of the preparations I made that morning. It immediately softens the tribulations of the day. It causes me to hasten through the chores I must get done before I can get into bed, and it encourages him to help me get them accomplished. The teamwork this preparation instills is magnificent. We find ourselves working for the same common goal: a wonderful night of making love.

I take my preparation a step further on those rare occasions when I have no pressing agenda, or if it happens to be a very special night, such as a birthday, an anniversary, or a celebration. For such special nights, I make a path with rose petals leading into the bedroom where I have set a small table dressed with my finest linens and china, candles and fresh flowers. Our favorite music plays softly in the background. The bed linens have been turned down and sprinkled with the fragrant petals for added romance. The room is aglow with strategically placed candles flickering in the soft breeze from the overhead fan. A special dinner is prepared, something light, capped off with a favorite dessert. No phones this night; conversation is enchanting, light, without interruption. No hurry, no rush, no pressing issues to attend. We have completely shut the world out. The night is ours.

These passionate memories are ones you'll recall with fondness, memories that will add depth to your relationship.

This is the spice of our sex life. With the busy lifestyles we lead, it can be difficult to set aside time for moments like these. Making such a priority preserves the intimacy of your marriage. It does require an extra measure of work and discipline on your part, but the rewards are immeasurable.

These passionate memories are ones you'll recall with fondness, memories that will add depth to your relationship, and memories that will build a history that will become the very fiber of your union. During moments of despair or turbulence, and all marriages face such times, you'll be able to draw from these memories and stand firm on the foundation built through your labor of love.

PAYBACK IS SWEET!

An added bonus for me was when my husband began to take the initiative to return the favor for special events, like Valentine's Day, my birthday, or a welcome-home time when I'd been away. It was gratifying to see the *tutorial efforts* taking root and actually bearing fruit to further enhance our marriage. A gentle reminder: *When your spouse is more important than you, you can never out-serve one another.*

You cannot effectively prepare the bed without the appropriate attitude. As we discussed earlier, you must be in the proper frame of mind; so *will* yourself into acting with an attitude of enthusiasm. The physical act of preparing the bed has launched the mindset. You have placed in his mind the anticipation of the night. If your husband leaves home for work before your bed is prepared, when he walks into the bedroom after getting home from a day's toil, the effect will be the same. Should he not venture into the room until bedtime, what a pleasant surprise will await him.

You have begun to prepare your mind, as well. I bustle through my day, rushing from here to there, but something usually triggers a recall about what I have planned for our night. It can either have a calming effect on me, or I must admit at the end of some days I'm thinking *I really wish I had put this night on hold*. When those days happen, no big deal. Herein lies the beauty of longevity in a relationship.

My husband usually, though not always (he is a man, you know) realizes it's been a horrific day for me. He suggests we just call it a night. His days are like that many times, as well, and then it becomes my suggestion to him. That's life. It can completely zap us of all energy and peace of mind at times, and as medicinal as sex can be to revitalize you, there are those times you will just want to pass. (Bet you're glad to know I'm human. You had probably really begun to dislike me by now!)

YOUR MOVE

The act of initiating is much of the lure in your sensual awareness. Sometimes we wives send confusing signals to our husbands that we just don't enjoy the physical act of sex. Whereas I will address this in more detail later, perhaps our men are reading us loud and clear.

Remember, sex is to be enjoyed by *both* spouses. If you're not thrilled with pleasing your husband, chances are you're not getting pleased. We have dealt with some principles that would be applicable here, and we will deal with others coming up.

At this juncture, I can only impress upon you to initiate sex often with your spouse. For myself, it is gratifying when I instigate our intimate moments, because my husband holds me in high regard and dotes on me every day. I love giving back to him in a way I know pleases him. Even though it benefits us both, he considers it a special gift. In his Promise Keepers vow to out-serve me, he makes me feel pretty special. What woman wouldn't love that?

Hopefully, your spouse is treating you with this same respect. However, if he falls short in this area, he needs to revisit the scriptures to discern what God teaches men about how to love their wives. This act of pleasing our husbands sexually is not entirely our responsibility; it takes two. It is easy to meet the needs of someone who loves you and makes you feel special day in and day out, and not just when he's feeling frisky. You may need to talk tenderly with your husband (perhaps during one of those candlelight dinners) about how you feel when he fails to love you as you deserve. Please understand, however, you will need to respond favorably to his attempts to alter his behavior. Changes in habit happen slowly, and the two of you will need to communicate to the other your recognition of the transformation.

7.
Play with Him

People talk about beautiful friendships between two persons of the same sex. What is the best of that sort, as compared with the friendship of a man and wife, where the best impulses and highest ideals of both are the same. There is no place for comparison between the two friendships; the one is earthly, the other divine."

MARK TWAIN

A CONNECTICUT YANKEE IN KING ARTHUR'S COURT

If you will, allow yourself to reminisce for a moment. Take yourself back in time, way back to puberty and remember the surprise and awe of your first attraction to the opposite sex. It seemed everyone had a boyfriend . . . except you. Competition was extremely heavy. You, like most of us, probably felt somewhat insecure in how you looked, how you handled yourself around boys, and could never quite get a handle on the rhythm of flirting. It seemed to come so easy for others, but it was somewhat awkward for you.

Then suddenly, along came *Mr. Right.* Your world was turned upside down. He noticed you. He winked at you. He brushed against your arm in the hall at school, and it sent shivers down your spine. Your mind was consumed with thoughts of him; you loved everything about him. You found yourself daydreaming about him, writing his name incessantly on your notebooks, anticipating your next encounter. When your eyes would meet, a feeling would well up inside of you and you thought you might burst with . . . with what? You didn't know, you couldn't explain it, you just knew it felt wonderful.

> *If courtship has died in your household, resurrect it today!*

Without realizing it at all, you made a flirtatious gesture to him. Your eyes met; yours sparkled. Your smile was timid; he loved it. You nervously gathered up your books; it was positive vibrations for him because he had managed to fluster you. The tease was on.

The tease was on, but then came the chase. We approached this folly in different ways. Some of us pursued; others of us played it aloof and were pursued. Regardless of the method, it was a chase.

Within the next few years, there were more opportunities to hone our skills and become well equipped for this game of love. Some of us never seemed to learn from our mistakes of love gone sour. Others learned to define explicitly the kind of mate with whom to share a lifetime commitment, and we would settle for nothing less.

The flirting, the chase, the capture, each shares one common element: it feeds the male ego. Men really have little to do with the ego issue; it is part of their makeup. I appreciate ego to a great degree; I simply have zero tolerance for overinflated ones. This thing called ego, however, is an essential, integral part of our men. Their virility is nourished by this fundamental component.

I love to watch my husband when his ego is being fed by me or others. His countenance becomes one of confidence, pride, and power. This is basically true for all of us. We enjoy being stroked, complimented, and believed in. It empowers us to a higher level of performance in whatever task is at hand.

This male ego follows us into the bedroom. How vitally important it is we nurture it. Teasing your mate adds to the intimate experiences you share. It sets the stage for your moments together, igniting the flame that must burn to keep solidity in your marriage. Teasing evokes spontaneity, which is essential to any sexual relationship.

COURTSHIP NEVER ENDS

After years of marriage, I flirt with my husband still, and he with me. When we call to check in during the day, we tease each other with sexual innuendoes that entice and excite us. It's a part of our courtship. Did I mention that? Courtship does not end when you get married. If it has died in your household, resurrect it today!

There are times when my husband is gone for an extended period of time. Whereas I do miss him during this time of separation, I find it can be refreshing. I grow again to appreciate the qualities in him I love the most, and recover from the irritations of those I don't. All husbands have them – those little annoying characteristics we'd like to change but have yet to alter in him. Knowing the gentle nature of my husband, he would never confess time away from me is equally as welcome, but I will readily admit I possess my own set of annoying traits.

While apart, we reflect on how life would be without the other. The reunion after a time of separation is very sweet. If your husband travels, make it a point to cause him to miss you while he's away. Temptation is not exclusive to traveling husbands (or wives), but the opportunity may present itself more often.

As often as I can, when I know my husband has an upcoming trip, I write love letters and/or cards before he actually departs. I mail them to his destination so that he has one waiting for him upon his arrival. He receives one every day he is gone. It means a lot to him to know I miss him, long for him, and await his return. I may date envelopes and place them in his suitcase, expecting him to open them on the appropriate dates. Or, when he's home, stick a note in his shirt pocket and designate a specific time to pull it out and read it during the day. It gives him a much-needed surge at just the right time, and you'll get a charge on the other end, as well.

I tease him in these notes. I talk about a specific memory we have made. I may only need to write one word that triggers a thought. He knows immediately what I mean. It's a very effective tool in the romance side of our marriage. We all have history we can draw from, and we should. These are the building blocks that continue to fortify and strengthen our relationship with our spouse.

Laughter is also a component of playing with him that he enjoys. Life can get so involved that we forget to mix it with a dose of laughter. Our husbands need this, and our children need to see us laugh together. How beneficial it is for you, as well. Laughter is medicinal, and it cures a lot of ailments around the home. You should make it a daily part of your routine.

Women come well equipped with the ability to flirt. It is a natural response. To some, it is a finely-tuned talent; others feel they have to work at it. You may feel you fit into the category of having to work at flirting, but if you are married or have captured a man's attention, you are obviously doing something right.

THE PHYSICAL TEASE

In a marriage, teasing can't end with verbal innuendoes, body language, or written contact. The most effective form of the tease is the physical. I know how much some women disdain it at times, but men love it—*grabbing and patting*. What is it that makes the physical tease so dynamic to our men? I don't know, but it must do something for them.

I have polled numerous women about *the grab* or *the pat* we get while standing at the sink doing dishes, walking out the door for work, bending over to pick up something, and sometimes for no reason at all. There are a few women who love it all the time; most are irritated by it some of the time. If your man is a grabber or patter, it must be a real charge, so let him have at it.

Once I adjusted my thinking on this, I no longer had the urge to deck my husband on those occasions when it irritated me. I understand this behavior is his way of teasing me, of sending a message of his desire for me, assuring me I still turn him on, even at the kitchen sink. I have learned to be very receptive to those grabs and pats, and it endears me to him even more.

What really bolsters him is when I grab back, and it's a plus when I grab first. This playful gesture assures him I'll take care of his need later, or *now* is as good a time as any if all conditions are right. It also reassures him I still find him attractive and desirable. So, go ahead, grab him. He'll love it.

SPICE OF TEASING

Has your husband ceased the physical tease with you? If so, why? Was it your response to the teasing? Has your marriage become so complacent that you're unresponsive to these gestures? Don't you miss it? Your marriage can become pretty bland without seasoning it with the spice of teasing. Why don't you initiate this part of your romance again? If he doesn't respond, check his pulse. He may be dead.

5.
Perform

Imagination is everything. It is the preview of life's coming attractions.

ALBERT EINSTEIN

Sex is no longer the *forbidden fruit*. You're married, remember? Lose your inhibitions. Set aside your timidity. Your performance can only be mastered when you become comfortable in the bedroom with your spouse. Through the years there has been an unfortunate stigma attached to sex, as I've touched on earlier, and many of us find we are captive to embarrassment about expressing our needs to our husbands. It is *acceptable* to talk about sex with your husband. In fact, it is the *right* thing to do.

Today, our society seems to be open about sex to the point of extreme promiscuity. By the mere fact our twelve-year olds are engaging in sexual encounters, one would automatically think it is just natural for us to broach the subject of what we like and what we don't, but this is far from the truth of the matter. In conversations with several young women who have been introduced to sex in this *free spirit* movement we have adopted as a society, I find they don't think men have changed much over the course of time. The women's story is always the same: "They want it all the time. I get so tired of having to please him, but he never knows how to please me. Do I ever get to say no? It's like he doesn't think there are two involved. It's all about him. I hate wham-bam-thank-you-ma'ams." Sound familiar? I repeat: some things never change.

When asked if they've discussed with their significant other about the problem of never getting satisfied sexually, they reply, "Why, no, I just can't say that to him."

"Why not?"

"Well, it's just something we don't talk about."

"Why not? Don't you talk about everything else?"

"Well, yeah, but I don't want to hurt his ego. You know how fragile that is."

The point is we're just too inhibited to express our desires in the bedroom. We're too inhibited to explore, to experiment with different ways and means and language; we remain content to have sex, make love, and that's that. Making love is an art, but in order to be a great artist you must lose any inhibitions you have about sex. For lovers, there is no room in bed for such restrictions.

LOSE YOUR INHIBITIONS

Okay, you're shy. So what? So am I about a few things. It takes practice. It takes *acting* – real acting sometimes. Most of us have dreamed of being an actress at some point in our lives. Well, here's your chance: act away. You can return to your timid self after you've made magic happen in the bedroom for you and your spouse. Behind closed doors with your husband can be a telltale time for the solidity and longevity of your marriage. Work on being comfortable with enjoying sex.

You'll never fully experience climactic ecstasy until you lose your inhibitions. Identifying why you have a lack of enthusiasm for sexual pleasure is imperative to dealing with this issue. Some of these issues have been addressed in other chapters. Anything from preconceived notions planted by parents or friends to medical matters and/or even some form of abuse may be plaguing you. Ask your husband to be patient as you work toward resolving this circumstance. I believe he'll be more than happy to wait it out knowing there may be greater rewards for both of you.

BE CREATIVE AND SPONTANEOUS

A great way to lose your inhibitions is to be creative in your sex life. Without going into great detail, don't be afraid of accumulating your personal items for romance along with candles, massage lotions, chocolate, fruit, roses, et cetera. If you're like most couples, you have a drawer devoted to your sexual activity. If not, set a goal to make it happen in your bedroom very soon. (Note: I am not a proponent of pornography in any form,

Behind closed doors with your husband can be a telltale time for the solidity and longevity of your marriage.

inside or outside the confines of the marital institution. I believe it is inherently wrong and serves only as a destructive and divisive tool in a healthy sex life.)

Conjure up meeting places. Designate a meeting time. Send an email (hopefully, the hackers won't intercept it!) and set the stage for the night. There's an endless list of new and refreshing ways to do something as old as . . . well, Adam and Eve. It takes a little thought and some effort to execute, but, oh, what flavor you'll add to your time together.

On several occasions I have kidnapped my husband from work. We steal away to a motel for the afternoon. He's onto me now. If I show up in a trench coat and heels, he's a little suspicious - especially if it's mid-July. I have been known to do the trench-heels flair at ballgames, or waiting for him in the parking lot after a game of golf. When he has been out of town, I occasionally will show up in my coat and heels at airports. (Nowadays, Homeland Security would have a big surprise waiting under the trench coat and I would be totally embarrassed, so that's the end of that.) You can certainly tell him you'll be waiting for him in the car at baggage claim. Then, sweep him away to a motel instead of home. Get his attention and yours on nothing but each other.

Too crazy, costly, risky, or bold for your imagination? Something that would totally embarrass your husband? Perhaps you think you know him well, but go ahead, try it. You both might be surprised at the results. Experiment with something less *crazy* and follow his lead; he may be more adventurous than you realized.

Healthy sexual appetites can be enhanced, or deterred, by the foods we ingest. Much of your spontaneity can depend upon your physical state or how easily you are to be stimulated. Proper exercise helps promote an active sex life. Arouse and excite your senses for sexual desire and pleasure by incorporating into your diet the omega-3 food group, dark chocolates, a good supplement of fish oil, and even Damiana tea. Take in less caffeine, as it is touted to be an inhibitor of sexual pleasure in women. When your mind is sluggish, creativity is stifled. Proper food groups and physical exercise provide the stamina necessary to maintain a vigorous bedtime demeanor.

Quickies Get the Job Done

I could never adequately emphasize the necessity for spontaneity in your sexual life. Those *quickies* we squeeze in just before the dinner guests arrive or before the children come home mean a lot. They have an edifying effect on each of us in different ways. It pumps up his ego; it is gratifying to me to know I was able to promote that. We find ourselves sending titillating glances across the room to each other all night. These little jump-starts keep our motors running while we're entertaining our guests. Cleaning up afterward is either at a stepped-up pace or put on hold till the next morning. The team effort was set in motion earlier, and carrying it through till the end – whenever those chores get done - becomes an enjoyable memory.

Whether spontaneous or planned encounters with your husband, you must entertain the thought often. The risk of not doing so is too costly. You cannot take for granted because he's not pressuring you for sex that he doesn't need it. My mother used to say, "If I have to ask somebody for something, I'd just as soon not have it. I want someone to give it to me because he or she loves me." How true. Be alert and watch for his *needy* signs. It may be as soon as the next morning after you've made mad, passionate love the night before. Just be there when he reaches out for you, and you do the reaching for him frequently. Believe me, he'll think you are the bee's knees!

The Wonder of It All

Remember pure love? Do you recall when you first fell in love with your husband? He was your greatest passion, your purest desire. It's a fundamental of a loving relationship. You gazed into his eyes and wanted to crawl inside his body via his tongue. You dated until curfew time, and afterward you talked on the phone for hours. You were together 15 hours a day, and it still wasn't enough. The wonder of love was an all-consuming fervor. That kind of love is a block of time all of us would love to rest in forever, but it stops for no one.

That place of reckoning of your devotion to him is the point in time you need to revisit frequently. I stressed the importance of this earlier. Your sexual performance hinges on this basic element. Evoke the passion you felt when life was simpler and love younger. Become starved for the explosion of love you shared "back when." Stirring those slumbering chords of romance will ignite your erotic senses, and you'll soon find you can't get enough of each other all over again.

Whatever you do, don't fall into a routine. Love-making should never be monotonous. Never settle for boredom.

Evoke the passion you felt when life was simpler and love younger.

I know there'll be those times when you have practically expended all the energy you have in a day, so you will be prone to settle for less than creative. Breathe life into your words and put yourself into your performance. You'll be amazed at how you will move from satisfaction to delight. Your whole motivation may be to satisfy his needs, move on to being satisfied yourself, but the end result will be sheer ecstasy for the two of you as you plunge to depths of love you have never sensed before. It's a very levitating emotion.

We are not super humans who can mass-produce electrical nights day in and day out. As a committed couple, however, you cannot allow yourselves to catch a rut. The danger of falling in a rut is it becomes habit. Take the lead and assume the responsibility. Strive to be whimsical, fun, adventurous and youthful in your lovemaking. You will soon find he will engage in the creativity and match your wits. It keeps the heat of passion more than lukewarm in your marriage.

YOU HAVE TO TRY

I will remind you: you are a woman. Women do what we have to do to accomplish a mission. I have assisted many wives in pulling their intimate lives out of the ruts of routine, and time and time again they praise the push out of their comfort zone.

Russell and Dana were high school sweethearts and were married while in college. Shortly after graduation, they had their first child. Russell took a job on the road; Dana worked and kept things going at home. Dana never has been keen on sex. She professed she always thought of it as *something dirty*; at least, that's how it was portrayed to her by her mother.

Russell became a little too lonely on the road and found pleasure through other means. Dana would talk about things Russell would do and say things didn't add up to her. Yet, she always defended him, wishing no one to feel any differently about him. He is a good man; he was just cheating on his wife. She became pregnant with their second child even during his unfaithfulness.

As I consoled Dana, she wanted me to help her win him back. He was content to *stay in* the marriage, but she *wanted* a vibrant relationship. I had been concerned over her perception of sex and had talked with her at great length on many previous occasions. Realizing everything else in her marriage was good, she would need to adopt a new way of thinking about sex and lose her inhibitions in order to please her husband. She decided she would make a sincere effort to win him back.

Now, before I go any deeper into this story, please realize I admire Dana's tenacity. Before my mother passed away, I could not tell someone at a funeral home who was crying over the loss of their mom that I, too, understood the loss they were feeling. I couldn't until now. I have never, knock wood, had to face the decision of what I would do if my husband was unfaithful. I will not even presume to have an idea. I do believe, however, it is an individual decision.

I have coached women who knew the marriage was over because they could never trust their husbands again. There are those, however, who fought for a man, and he stayed, and their marriage was stronger than ever before. There are also those who have stayed in the marriage, and one or the other, or both, have never forgiven the act, and they are absolutely miserable. Staying in a marriage when your spouse has breached your trust is a personal decision, and I admire the people who can go the distance with forgiveness. I pray I would be able to do the same.

The sacrifice was for herself, her family, and God.

Meanwhile, Dana decided to *spice up* her act a bit. She sought my advice, and we discussed her sexual inhibitions. We spent a day visiting *Victoria's Secret*, various body lotion stores, and she even purchased a manual on sex. By day's end, we had managed to season her bedroom with many dynamics for her new approach to intimacy. We went through the advice outlined in this book. She developed a new pattern of thinking about pleasing him. She would call him on the road and plant innuendoes in his mind for coming-home celebrations. She left notes in his suitcase, tucked away others in the pockets of his shirts and pants. She became very creative in her surprises for him when he would come home after a two-week jaunt on the road. It took time and effort on her part, but Dana was fighting for the man she loved. She would fight and pray, she decided, until he would call it quits. She had nothing to lose and everything to gain.

I am happy to report that Dana won. It worked. They are the happiest lovebirds you'll meet anywhere. The past is the past for her; it is never mentioned. They only have a great future to look forward to. Accolades to Dana for her staying power. It took guts, determination and perseverance. The sacrifice she made was not just for herself, but for her family and for God. She fully understands the meaning of commitment.

Dana is quick to give credit for the recovery of her marriage to her establishment of a healthy intimate relationship with her husband. She appreciates the advice on being creative in the bedroom, and contends that she had a skewed perception of the sexual act. She has now come to enjoy the physical act as much as Russell. She has surprised herself with her performance, and they have grown to find the chemistry that drew them together years ago.

FOREPLAY, A CRUCIAL ELEMENT

Foreplay is an ingredient that should never be left out of your lovemaking experience, and shouldn't necessarily originate at bedtime. All of the teasing, the flirting, the pinching and grabbing, the pausing in between washing a dish or putting clothes in the laundry for a prolonged sensuous kiss and embrace . . . foreplay. These expressions communicate to your husband you are ready for a time of great sex. They communicate to him your need for the tenderness and caresses that will ensue. The language sends the message to him of how important his role is in your fulfillment and enjoyment. Your pre-foreplay encounters are stimulating, and they encourage a more intimate time of foreplay in the bedroom.

Impress upon your husband how important foreplay is to you as a woman. Women usually need some down time to unwind before hopping into the act of making love. We gals have difficulty turning off the day's events. Convince your spouse how his teasing sets the stage and prepares your heart for love. The number one complaint of women I have coached with regard to lack of sexual fulfillment: there is no affection or tenderness prior to the request for sex. Remind him he holds the key to ensuring that you first *engage* and then *share* in the pleasure of this special time together.

Don't forget to make part of your foreplay a refreshing shower or relaxing bath. Then, slip into something *more comfortable*. Come on, invite him into the shower or Jacuzzi with you. Lather up each other. Follow each other's contours as you tantalize and excite your senses. Sometimes I love my man sweaty, right off the lawnmower or the golf course. But most of the time, there's nothing like clean, fresh skin that gets me going. He splashes on my favorite cologne. I put on his favorite fragrance. We take in deep breaths and allow our senses to be aroused.

Concerted efforts of setting the stage for love can, and should, become habitual in your intimate life. It's a regimen that becomes your attitude, and it's your attitude that becomes a regimen. Making sexual advances to your husband should be as naturally a part of your day as dressing for work, getting the kids off to school, or eating. A good-morning kiss, a pat on his behind, a tender stroke of his face, a straight-on connection with his eyes gets your attention focused on each other for the day. These forms of foreplay need to be incorporated regularly as part of your love life. Remember: tuck a little note in his money clip, wallet, shirt or pants pocket. He'll be sure to find it during the course of his busy day. Memorialize how much you

...you know the language he loves

love him, how you plan to show him you do when he gets home. Anything you want to say; you know the language he loves. The important thing is that you drive home the history of love you two continue to make in your marriage. It is this history you pull from daily life that causes you to know why you love him so dearly. It's the special times you have shared thus far. Your history needs to be good, steadfast, and worth revisiting.

TAKE ALL THE TIME YOU NEED

Rushing through tenderness with those we love most is a mistake many of us make in our marriages, so don't feel like the Lone Ranger if you are guilty in this area. Mornings are hectic at everyone's house. Afternoons and nights are slammed with activities. You really have to be mindful of keeping important things like hugs, kisses, and I-love-you moments top priority for you, him, and your children. You must never forget the urgency of him thinking only of you when he steps out your door into his world. It is forever urgent. Failing in this department is how complacency slides through the cracks, and we begin taking our marriage for granted.

Your history needs to be good, steadfast, and worth revisiting.

His world is probably one devoid of your physical presence during the day. Make sure you are ever present in his heart and mind. It is your responsibility to ensure you have stirred his desires sufficiently before you separate for your day's activities. He'll only think of getting back to you that evening. It is a practice you must perform every day, because if you send him on his way feeling neglected and taken for granted, temptation's foot may just kick the door wide open. Many times, it happens just that quickly.

NEVER COMPARE

As discussed earlier, comparing lovers is one of the most demeaning and damaging mistakes you can commit in making love. This dilemma is another reason why parents need to teach abstinence to their kids. Exposure to several sexual partners over the years carries with it more risks than STDs. The comparison quandary has beset many marriages over the years. The onslaught of swingers is a trend that will come back to haunt the hundreds that applaud its "benefits."

I can assure you, God does not honor behavior of this nature in marriages. I personally have witnessed the demise of several marriages that have assumed this sort of sexual impropriety. It has not only destroyed these people's marriages, it has caused tremendous damage to their children's perception of relationships. The couples have gone their separate ways and emotionally and/or physically now struggle with sexual deficiencies in some form or another. My earnest prayer is you *never* engage in a swinging episode. It is simply too costly - here on Earth and later on.

Your performance hinges on your monogamy of mind. It's difficult to focus on what to praise about him if you're replaying encounters from past relationships. Comparing out loud, or silently, is costly in your marriage. Why go there? If you are the one who had a previous encounter, you may be dealing with how your partner compares to someone else. If your partner is the one who had a previous encounter, you may be dealing with how you compare to his experiences. It can become quite testy at best. Some things are best left unspoken, and this definitely falls within that category.

Don't ask, don't tell. Don't even let your thoughts return to that time zone. Don't compare. Remember, you are working on making your marriage a unique and fulfilling experience with its own memories. It is your distinctive history. Don't let a third party invade your private gathering.

PRAISE HIS EFFORTS

A huge plus for your performance in bed will be acknowledging your husband's response to your requests. Remember to praise him for the things he does that are good and just right in your love-making. Talk each other through what feels good. Guide each other's hands to every erogenous zone. Then commend him on a job well executed. He needs to hear reaffirmation when he pleases you.

It is equally important to let one another know when something isn't good. Hopefully, he'll make mental note of it. If he forgets, remind him again – through tenderness, not frustration. (I'll deal with other means of rein-

Your spouse cannot fulfill you if he doesn't know how.

forcement in the Train Him chapter.) Once they sense your lack of response to certain advances, they will focus more on what does elicit stimulation.

Don't be shy about telling him what works and what doesn't. Just as communication is an integral part of each facet of everyday life, it has no less value in the bedroom. Your spouse cannot fulfill you if he doesn't know how. Keep a positive attitude, open your heart, mind and will, lay aside your inhibitions, and then . . . perform.

THINK LIKE A MAN

A distinctive quality our men possess is how they can instantly turn off their emotions at the first thought of sex. It rarely matters how difficult their day has been, what burdens may be heavily weighing on their heart and mind, or even that they are presently at odds with their wives over some issue. They can tune the world out and lay everything else aside for sexual release.

Women are not designed this way. Don't you wish we

were? Owning a business has helped me to think in a more black-and-white way, and I take pride in exercising that trait when it comes to our intimacy. My experience has been once I relinquish my emotions and allow him to take me away, I find it is exactly what I need. At times, this exercise will take some mind-over-matter thinking. This, again, is where the mindset of sex becomes important. Your attitude must be adjusted. You will need to exercise complete control of your feelings, i.e., put them on hold, and redirect your train of thought to loving your man. It is not easy to separate that natural part of being a woman and set aside a day's events. After enough practice at instantly changing from drive to reverse, it will become second nature for you as you come to enjoy gearing up for sex at will.

EVEN, AND ESPECIALLY, DURING ADVERSITY

Today's families seem to be facing onslaughts of adversity in various forms, but illnesses can be devastating. Ministers' families deal day in and day out with couples who have serious medical conditions within their immediate family unit, and oftentimes involving a minor child. This misfortune can take a tremendous toll on a couple. We have witnessed countless incidents where the marriages have not lasted, even if the child recovers from an apparently terminal illness. The odds of divorce greatly increase with the death of a child.

It is sad to witness couples who have not guarded their relationship to withstand difficulties such as these. These conditions call for extraordinary measures of patience, understanding, strength, comfort and love between the parents. And, yes, especially intimacy.

It seems natural to put your entire life on hold during traumatic circumstances, and some aspects of people's lives do come to a screeching halt. When faced with these situations, a family can experience blowouts in many aspects of life, and typically a temporary patch is the only remedy readily available. A mother's heart beckons her to focus her entire attention on the child who desperately needs her. With multiple children in the picture, she must continue to struggle with meeting the others' needs. Families who have mastered the art of teamwork adapt to these types of changes much easier than those who are disjointed. Fathers who have accepted responsibilities and appropriate leadership within the household can make this new transition within the family an adjustment that doesn't get out of control.

Countless times, however, I have witnessed mothers neglect the needs of their husbands during these unfortunate seasons in life. The men tend to get lost in the shuffle of the disarray and often find themselves wearing a patch over essential needs, especially intimacy. Some have sought advice from me on how best to approach their wives about remembering to love them, as well. When they even so much as make a hint of making love, their wives go off on them and cause them to feel guilty about their suggestion. Stressful medical conditions can sometimes drag on for years, and wives tend to relegate sex to the very bottom of their things-to-do list. It is the last thing on their minds, and they believe their husbands should feel the same way.

Hear ye! Hear ye! **His sexual needs don't stop**. While most husbands are willing to put their desires on hold for several weeks and even months, after a while it becomes crucial to them to be redeemed. It is not just the sexual release that is so important to him; it is the need for affection and tenderness. This release is equally as important to the woman's well-being.

Sadly, I have witnessed adverse periods in couples' marriages end in divorce. They made it through the illness to the end. Sometimes it ended in death; sometimes the illness was overcome. The neglect of each other throughout the struggle left them with no bond at the end of the day. Their faith brought them through the battle, but once the dust settled, they found their love for each other had been lost somewhere along the way.

Phil and Tina were a terrific couple. Their marriage was fabulous, and seemingly unshakable. Childhood leukemia plagued their nine-year-old daughter. She fought a great fight, but went on to be with her Lord. Mom and Dad were naturally broken-hearted, and were there for each other for even a few years after Jodi's death. Tina could not let go of the emotional trauma in order to meet Phil's needs. Night after night she turned her back and left him frustrated, hurt and angry. Her neglect of his sexual desires brought the demise of their marriage. He was starved for affection, and eventually found it from someone else.

Bob and Brenda were more fortunate. . .in some respects. Tommy lived. It was a speedy recovery, but even so, the stress was too much for Brenda. She was constantly in fear of the return of the cancer, and completely wrapped herself up in Tommy's life. Their marriage had not experienced the depth it should have, and a very hasty end found its way into their lives. Tommy was 21 when diagnosed. He is married and rearing his own family now. Brenda is miserable. Embittered by the divorce, she lives in denial that her neglect of Bob played any role in his finding refuge in the arms of another woman.

Embraces, affection, sexual intimacy are crucial to both parties in times of medical pressures and other impositions within the family unit. It is a given that these times will be difficult, but when they have passed, whatever timetable that happens to be, the history you have developed between each other prior to the occurrence, as well as during, will govern the history you make in the future. You must never lose sight of the importance of being there for him, even when your heart is heavily burdened. You will draw strength from each other and be able to face the most difficult of days.

DON'T STOP CARING

I've had many men ask me why wives stop trying to satisfy a man's sexual needs. Do they forget? Stop caring? What exactly is it? It's a valid issue. Women seem to lose sexual desire for their husbands. We tend to take it for granted he's going to love us, be committed and stick around forever just because he should. Some do; others don't. Ask the countless number of women who fall victim to infidelity just how blind-sided they are when they get the news. Even the ones who *suspect* things *aren't quite right* are still devastated with the circumstances following the announcement that *he doesn't love me anymore.*

I tend to place most women in three categories: those on the prowl for sex, those in hibernation from sex, and those of us who are in the middle and like to stay there – we're willing when he is and initiating sex, as well. The middle-grounders are few and far between. The women on the prowl take advantage of the husbands whose wives are hibernating.

It happens. Women begin taking their marital relationships for granted very soon after marriage. We do everything we can to hook our man, and once we snag him, we do little else to keep him on the hook. Life gets in the way. Children come along and divert our attention. Marriages become stale. Our husbands haven't measured up to our expectations. We're too tired, too stressed, too fat, too flatchested, too mad, too sad, too depressed, too dirty, too clean, too selfish, or it's just too much trouble. All this can add up to too little too late! He can become too distracted for you. This distraction can come in the form of another woman, pornography, or other avenues of release.

Sex *is* important to him. Flash: It will probably *always* be important to him. We cannot stop meeting his needs. Remember: our sexual performance must become one of habit. Sex should be a nourishing element in our lives. Like a good, healthy diet and exercise, it should be a consistent routine. When we eat well, we feel well. When we're exercising, we feel full of energy. When people get out of the habit of going to church, it's difficult to get in the swing of regular attendance again. Satisfying the sexual appetite of our husband is just as important to the health of our marriage as keeping a healthy financial plan. Anytime we reduce the frequency of nourishing elements in our lives, our position changes.

We don't like it when our men look at other women, whether on the street or on the television screen. We don't want them to get *worked up* over someone else, but we don't want to *work them up* ourselves. It's unfair to expect husbands to have that sort of self-control if wives are not willing to do their part in the bedroom. I know God expects self-control of your husband, and so do you, but you must bear in mind: he is only human, and humans fail every day.

Again, I realize there are men who have a problem with *lust.* This can spoil a wife's desire to perform sexually. I know some men who even make remarks to their wives about *endowments* of other women. It's not enough that they howl over the lusted-after woman, but they turn around and demean and belittle their wives. What's a woman to do?

If your husband has these tendencies, what do you do? You can't shoot him; you still have to love him. Behavior like this can cause you to feel very insecure, and it presents another issue within the realm of communication that must be addressed. If you are able to communicate to your husband how his remark makes you feel, how it disengages your desire to please him, you two should be able to come to an understanding. If he ceases his behavior and witnesses a firsthand response to your appreciation of his having done so, this should make for a much better emotional state for you. You do care that he is making love to you instead of some *honey* he lusted over earlier, so don't try to convince yourself you don't. Tackle the problem head on, but have a plan based on the principles you've worked through thus far.

> *As wrong as it feels, husbands don't always wait until you've caught up with life.*

Loving your husband simply cannot be something you stop caring about. He may have stopped showing care and concern for you, and you most likely have tried to correct it through various means. What I continue to impress upon couples is the fact that when your love-life is out of sync, everything in your marriage seems to be that way. This thing called intimacy, this natural desire God placed within you to be needed, to be loved, to be fulfilled sexually is vital to the nurturing of your relationship to your husband. It cannot be put off for a more convenient season in your life. As wrong as it feels, husbands don't always wait until you've caught up with life.

MAKE YOUR EXERCISE COUNT

Your performance is incredibly enhanced by staying physically fit. I conveyed the importance of fitness in the chapter about looking great for your husband. It plays equally as important a role in your physical performance in the bedroom. Through the years, I have talked with a great number of married men who have found sexual pleasure with a younger woman. My curiosity found me querying them as to why the youthfulness. I attribute my interest in attempting to find some validation to this question in large part to Willie Nelson's and Waylon Jennings' song "Luckenbach, Texas" and their intriguing line about "firm-feeling women." Let's face it: men love firmness! Yes, we are very much aware that they, too, sag as they age, but my observation has been that if you have a woman who is conscious about her health, it usually suffuses the life of her spouse. (Again, there are exceptions to every rule.)

You won't always be able to keep your firmness, so you must ensure that you sufficiently enamor him with your abilities in bed to keep him coming back to you for his needs. It is likewise vital for you to remain confident and secure about yourself and not allow negative feelings about your changing body to interfere with the healthiness of your love relationship with your husband. The depth of love that the two of you create will be each other's security blanket as the years defy the laws of gravity.

And then, naturally, there's the performing like a twisted pretzel act that our men expect of us. I've often thought about applying with the Cirque du Soleil as one of their contortionists. You know the ones; they tie themselves up in knots and turn themselves inside out and never break a sweat. Amazing! Flexibility. You gotta love it! And you wish you'd never lost it because it surely could come in handy at times. I would encourage you to keep up that muscle dexterity as much as possible. If you strive never to lose it as a young person, it's easier to keep it up the older you become. It enhances every area of your life, not to mention your lovemaking.

I find it somewhat self-serving, particularly when I'm out on the playground with my grandkids. Parents sitting watching as their children play are intrigued as I'm crawling through the ground tunnels, hopping over the tire obstacle courses, climbing over and through and around the jungle gyms, sliding down the tunnel slides, and pulling myself up on the monkey bars. Before I know it, most of the kids in the park have joined in on the fun of my chasing them around like a crazy person. It's thrilling for my grandkids, and it does me good to know that I'm still capable of some quick moves in tight places!

Maintaining strength and stamina for active love-making has enormous benefits. Your flexibility will serve you well in assuming favorite positions and taking some of the load of responsibility off your husband. While the

> *Engage with energy; enjoy with ecstasy.*

activity is good for his heart, we need to pull our fair-share load in the physical department. Plunging ourselves into the appetites of the body intensifies our pleasure. Staying fit is the key to ensuring you can hang in there for the exquisite pleasure that awaits you.

Perhaps one of the saddest comments I have heard from men who have been unhappy in their wife's sexual performance has been that they feel as though they're making love to a corpse. You get the picture? Don't make me have to spell it out! It is tragic when meeting our husband's needs becomes a matter of the last item on our to-do list for the day, and we want it over with so we can get about our sweet slumber. Engage with energy; enjoy with ecstasy.

DO IT OFTEN

Yes, do it often. *The more you do it, the more you do it,* to borrow a quote from my husband. (He was not preaching about sex at the time, but it is befitting.) This is true in any habit you strive to maintain: prayer, exercise, diet, sex.

It is good to adopt a routine of sex, as I discussed earlier. You feel happier. Your relationship feels solid and you are secure in that, therefore, life is easier to handle. You feel healthier. If you engage in the physical act as you should, it increases your breathing and you are working lots of muscles. It is a cardiac workout. This may be the only form of exercise many of you get, so keep it up.

Your body responds to sex for multitudes of reasons. It causes you to remember; it causes you to forget. After particularly good love-making, perhaps you have realized nothing else mattered while you were in the act. All the burdens of the world seemed to have vanished for a while. You completely focused on each other. What a great release. You feel better equipped to handle anything that comes your way.

SEX IS MEDICINAL

We may not understand why the physical act of sex makes us feel good, but there are biological reasons. Helen Fisher, Ph.D., and author of *Why We Love, The Nature and Chemistry of Romantic Love,* explains that women who regularly receive semen vaginally are less depressed than those who don't.

Semen is supplied with testosterone and estrogen, as we are all aware. Do you realize, however, it also contains chemicals such as dopamine and norepinephrine, serotonin, and oxytocin. These all can contribute to either euphoria or tranquility. When we achieve orgasm, the oxytocin and vasopressin that is released promote feelings of contentment and attachment.

The more you do it, the more you do it . . . because you need it. Never think of it as a chore or something only for him. This physical act of sex is intended for your pleasure and benefit, also. As I mentioned previously, the amount of pleasure you receive may be dependent upon your open and frank discussions with your husband about what makes you feel good. Remember, sex is not the forbidden fruit in your relationship. You are married to this man, and you have committed to keeping his pants on until he gets home.

9.
Train Him

A woman worries about the future until she gets a husband.
A man never worries about the future until he gets a wife.
AUTHOR UNKNOWN

Natural chemistry between a man and a woman is precious. It truly is the first sign of love. Erotic pleasure can be attainable with a little chemistry in a relationship. Most married couples can claim some chemistry, at least at the beginning of their relationship. There are those couples whose love spawned from first being friends. The passion which glues us in our first years of marriage is something that must be kept intact in order to maintain quality in our sexual relationship, as well as in our day-to-day life.

There is no guarantee, even with chemistry, our partner will know how to bring us to the height of ecstasy desired when making love. We must assume the role of *teacher* in our bedroom. We each bring our unique idiosyncrasies into marriage. I like neat; he's a slob. I eat grilled; he eats fried. I'm a morning person; he's not. I squeeze the toothpaste tube at the bottom; he just squeezes. Living together only works with compromise. Happy couples develop a system workable for both.

Through much trial and error, you and your husband made adjustments to each other's peculiarities. Compromises are the norm for newlyweds. Few escape the surprise of nonconformity on one or the other's part. It oftentimes is a battle of wills in who will surrender to the but-honey-I've-always-done-it-this-way plan. But, the bumps usually smooth out as one party gives in and moves on. These situations are how we learn what makes the other tick. It is the discovery of how far we can push, just what our boundaries are, and how benevolent our hearts are willing to be. You both are exploring and uncovering characteristics and mannerisms that perhaps have never surfaced before. It is the launch of our training process in our marriage. This process is one where you both assume the role of trainer and trainee. It's how we learn to live with those we love.

KEEPING SCORE NEVER WINS IN THIS GAME

Women's psychological nature gets us in over our heads at times. We dissect his every move, every word, every thought. We won't let things go. We keep score. We keep past grievances buried just beneath the surface. That way, when we find some reason to be upset with him again, we don't have to dig too deeply to pick another bone or two with him. And at just the right time of the month, we go for the jugular. Without any warning, we have had his lunch and cleaned his plate all in one fell swoop. It doesn't take a man very long to figure out that he needs to avoid trouble in paradise. The more tender-hearted, gentle-spirited men learn to tip-toe around us, busy themselves with projects sure to make us happy, and to become super accommodating to our wants and wishes. The more selfish, mean-spirited men can send their wives into tailspins and/or keep them with broken, contrite spirits. This scenario usually makes for unhappy times, and if not reined in can develop into serious disturbances.

Regardless of the personalities of you and your husband, your marriage is a work in progress. You each will learn the buttons you should push and those you shouldn't. You also can become skilled at how to please, down to preparing his favorite meals. These exercises are essential in providing insight for delving into your spouse's heart and keeping a pulse on his basic needs. The ideal development is that he, likewise, strives to please you.

I always enjoyed watching couples play "The Newlywed Game" or "The Dating Game." (Yeah, yeah, I know, it dates me somewhat.) It was always interesting to see who knew the most facts about his or her spouse. Some couples felt really inept as to how uninformed they were about little things regarding their spouse. It thrilled me for the ones who were tuned in to each other. It was obvious they had logged in on familiarity of their mates. The exchange of eye-twinkling satisfaction defined the nurturing relationship.

The great majority of the time, it will be the woman who pays attention to the details. I appreciate God instilling that quality in us. It's definitely one of our finer traits. I will readily admit, however, that my husband usually prevails over me in those games. He knows all the particulars about me. It makes me feel really good to know that he pays attention to what makes me unique. He has to stay on his toes, however, because in keeping with a woman's trademark, I change on a whim. It keeps life interesting.

Our marriage, as does yours, has a style. It takes on a

personality all its own. Your marriage has its individual mannerisms. You develop a response to certain situations. You react to comments, glances and touches, and you may react in a completely different manner at one time over another. Your husband is no different from a child putting his hand to a hot stove. If your response burns him one day, he may not risk the pain the next.

Your bedroom manner will develop an exclusive style, as well. Men will attain satisfaction; you can count on it. Once again, depending on the personality of your husband, he may pay close attention to details of your response to his touch. If you are like most women, some days a certain caress is just what you need to arouse you; other days the same touch sends you spiraling. Men have a difficult time trying to form any kind of pattern to your likes and dislikes. If your mood directs your cravings, you may find you will need to direct and instruct him each time you make love on how to bring you to your much-desired climax.

If your response burns him one day, he may not risk the pain the next.

This special time you share as a couple is a training session. It is an exercise that keeps you fit for love. Your basic training will equip your marriage for good times and bad times. You will be able to face the hard times and keep love intact, and the prosperous times will be even sweeter. You are in training to prepare yourself for the feeling of complete comfort with your spouse. Knowing him inside out, realizing what makes him tick, giving him insight into how to stimulate you, and striving to please him in everything you do are sure ways to keep his heart tuned to yours.

Honey-Do-Me List

The *honey-do list* is terminology every married man understands. Much of the time, it's an ethereal list at best—in their heads and in light-hearted conversation with their peers. My honey-do list is rarely written down for my husband, although he would prefer it be memorialized and spelled out definitively. It's an ongoing, run-on list that is indelibly present in my mind, and I can recite the items left to be done at any given moment. I believe some of the tasks left still to be completed on his honey-do list date back to five years ago. He'll strike them off someday, and when he does, both of us will rejoice. He is always pleased when he accomplishes one of the myriad projects I have mapped out for him.

I am not in the yacht alone. You have your list, I'm quite certain, and it most likely has a history as well. The problem with the honey-do list is that if we're not careful, we are mistakenly viewed as nagging. I pride myself in *gently reminding* him about tasks to be done, and he half-heartedly agrees that's the spirit intended. I truly believe our husbands get a real charge out of the age-old tale of the nagging wife, and I tend to let those comments roll off the ol' back.

There's good reason why he prefers the itemization of the tasks I have for him. Your husband would likely identify with his rationale. He doesn't enjoy reading my mind, and he's really never mastered the art. So if I want it done my way, it's best I spell it out with specificity.

Guess what? The same concept applies in the bedroom. I call it the *honey-do-me list.* My list, again, is not written down, but I do spell out for him how I want him to make love to me. I quickly learned that he couldn't read my mind in this department either, and if I was going to get satisfied and enjoy it to its fullest, I simply had to give him a honey-do-me list. It worked! Yes, sometimes I have to remind him about an item on the list. Imagine that; he forgets! We laugh about it, and he responds, "Women never forget, and men never remember." (Hey, he said it first.) But, just like a honey-do list, he'll take care of it. He wants nothing more than to please me. That's why he checks off my honey-do list of projects around the home, and that's why he makes sure he keeps me satisfied in the bedroom. He fully understands the concept of *when mama ain't happy, ain't nobody happy.*

Present your husband with your honey-do-me list. If he has a true heart for pleasing you, I guarantee you he'll *get 'er done.* In order to create your list, you must be fully aware of how you want to be loved by him. You must be able to explicitly lead him through motions, or notions, of what pleases you most. Give him a list of ways you enjoy him touching you, where you want to be caressed, even how you want to be kissed.

Sounds simple, doesn't it? It is. He is your soulmate. Remember? You see each other naked all the time. It's okay to talk about what makes you feel sensually aroused.

Coach him as to a better way to make love to you. Making demands doesn't produce the desired results, nor does getting frustrated when he can't read your mind. You cannot assume he should know what you desire and how you desire it. *You must tell him.* But, don't forget the tip about praise, which we discuss in the upcoming chapter. Just like children, we all need kudos for what we do right. The constructive criticism doesn't sting as deeply when they feel they've brought some sense of pleasure to you. If you haven't grown comfortable discussing your likes and dislikes regarding sex, this training may be difficult for you. The more we practice at something, the easier it becomes. It will soon be as natural for you to talk about sensitive matters in your sex life as it is to talk about what you want for dinner.

YOU KNOW HIS HEART

I would surmise that you had a general idea of your husband's selfish nature or, hopefully, lack thereof long before you married him. You might be surprised how many women have no idea they managed to snag a self-centered egotistical *jerk*. If your man has a tender heart, a heart for you who he promised to love and to cherish, he will readily accept guidance from you in order to bring you sexual fulfillment.

If your husband is a Christian, you are ahead of the game in having a great marriage. Whether you have been in your marriage one year or forty, he is committed to you at this moment. You want to ensure his commitment holds firm and you are the one feasting on his love. Malnutrition is never acceptable in this incomparable aspect of your marriage. When you work on training each other about what turns you on and begin to incorporate many *work-out* sessions, you safeguard your marriage against an unwelcome invasion.

10.
Praise Him

"It's just too hot to wear clothes today," Jack said as he stepped out of the shower. "Honey, what do you think the neighbors would say if I mowed the lawn like this?"
"Probably that I married you for your money," she replied.
AUTHOR UNKNOWN

WE THRIVE ON PRAISE

Each of us requires affirmation and approval. It is important to keep a positive attitude in order to maintain good mental and physical health. When we receive confirmation and praise for a job well done, it drives us to perform with excellence. It inspires us to reach our goals. We have a great need to share these accomplishments with someone we love. To receive a gesture of approval from an employer or coworker is a feeling of great satisfaction, but it pales in comparison to the approval we receive from our spouses.

What a boost to your husband's ego when you remember to tell him how handsome he looks. He needs affirmation from you as much as you need it from him. He needs to feel you are still physically attracted to him. He enjoys hearing a particular color becomes him. He wants verification his jeans suits his body. Let him know his cologne fills your senses. He must feel you melt in his embrace when your eyes meet. He seeks approval of his appearance, as well as for his accomplishments.

All too often when my husband and I have comforted hurting couples, it appears a large part of their suffering comes from a lack of appreciation. Many spouses feel taken for granted when there is no positive reinforcement for anything they do. Frequently, the problem stems from a lack of communication and/or expression of gratitude for the efforts put forth by one or both parties.

...there is always someone willing to shower [him] with praise and adoration.

We all must hear the words. It is affirming contentment to us when our mate is proud of us, notices what we do, how we do it, how often it's done, what we wear, how we look, believes in us, and acknowledges our accomplishments.

IF YOU DON'T PRAISE HIM, *SHE* WILL

One may be a success as a parent, as a friend, and as a professional, but when a spouse gives no accolades for these accomplishments, everyone else's approval seems diminished. We run a risk of exposing our relationships to infidelity, because there is always someone willing to shower our spouse with praise and adoration. If we don't take note, some other woman will.

A friend of mine shared with me how unhappy he had been for the past several years in his marriage. His wife, who used to do everything with him, found no enjoyment even in going to dinner, much less going for a golf game or a boat ride or to an amusement park, or even vacation. When they married, she was very thin and attractive. She was still attractive, but had gained a significant amount of weight. He felt guilty that he desired her to weigh less. He longed for her to get back to a slimmer, healthier look. Naturally, he knew he could not expect her to be as slim as when she started out in their marriage, because she had had several children along the way. He just wanted her to stay fit. He had offered encouragement to launch her enthusiasm in losing weight, even to walk with her or exercise with her. She would never stick with the program. She was moody, depressed, angry, bitter, frustrated, and completely unmotivated.

He had a demanding job, one that afforded his family an elaborate lifestyle. His wife, however, never seemed satisfied with his accomplishments. Either he wasn't making enough money, which would require him to spend more time at the office, or if he spent the time at the office in order to make more money, she was unhappy because he was never home.

He had tried everything to please her. He helped with the kids, the laundry, the cooking, the gardening, and even did the finances of the home while giving her free rein of the checkbook. He looked for solace at home after a hard day's work, but would find he came up empty almost every day. While he admitted that she would actually be pleasant some of the time and he would feel as though they were breaking down the walls, something would snap two days later. She would soon be back to treating him with disrespect and spewing resentful comments. Equally bad, he found that she would make demeaning remarks to her family and friends about him.

He pleaded with her to talk with him, to explain what he could do to make things better. How could he cause her to lose her memory of the injustice he had brought upon her in a moment of betrayal? He had found comfort in the arms of someone who seemed to offer everything she wouldn't, someone who believed in him and praised him for his accomplishments, and someone who built up his ego at every level. This new lover made him feel like a man! It would be a relationship he would not remain in because he realized the stakes. He had made a commitment and would honor God and his family by staying in the marriage.

Even though years had passed, it was apparent that he had not forgiven himself any more than his wife had for his weakness in the flesh. The matter was a constant throw-it-in-your-face topic in times of conflict, which became more frequent than not in their marriage.

As I sat and listened to the laundry list of disgruntlements, my heart ached for my friend. He obviously felt he was at the end of his rope with the marriage. Try as he may, she was never happy and had never thanked him for his accomplishments. I saw a man's heart longing for life. He was dying inside. His heart was one that loved God, one that had a sense of moral obligation and responsibility. His was a heart that cared deeply for his children's welfare and well-being. It was a heart hardened toward his wife.

My friend's heart was one that needed praise from his spouse. He was wearing his ego down around his knees! He was a very accomplished man, a lover of life, one who was friend to all. This great man could never recondition his wife's thinking or actions toward him.

His spirit was one of brokenness that would eventually drain him of all self-dignity, self-respect, self-esteem, and self-motivation. As soon as the children were grown and gone, he moved on to a life without his spouse. His wife was in disbelief that once they had the house to themselves, he had decided it was too small for just the two of them. It was move on or continue to live a meaningless, discouragement-filled life. He had lived out that scenario far too many years. He chose to live without her.

My friend was willing to live with his wife's weight gain, although it was not his preference. He said he could even cope with the anger and bitterness she felt in her unforgiving spirit. After all, he felt he deserved the punishment. The one thing he could not cope with and, eventually, refused to accept was the constant berating of his ego, and the lack of gratefulness for the provider he had been for the family. It was the straw that ultimately broke his will and led him to a refuge of solitude.

THAT WONDERFUL MALE EGO

As much as women may profess to disdain that male ego, it is the driving force behind what makes a man strive to please his family. Stroking his ego is essential in maintaining a positive self-image for your man. Praise your husband. Encourage everything he does. Yes, he has his faults, but he's yours. None of us is perfect, including you. Find the positive in all he does. It causes him to aspire to excellence to please you. It makes you feel better about what he does, as well. This sounds very basic and similar to how we treat our children. Adults are just grown-up children. No one ever outgrows the need for affirmation and praise.

The male ego is the driving force behind what makes a man strive to please his family.

Women can be very critical. We must be vigilant in our

encouragement of our men. When they try to do something that pleases us, even if it doesn't meet our expectations, we must praise them for their efforts. Even if they fall short in pleasing our romantic needs, when an attempt is made, boast of their efforts. Women read an enormous number of romance novels a year. Our perception of what will satisfy our need for living out a fantasy can become somewhat askew. Praise them, yes, even when they fall short.

Women must also keep in mind that many times their men didn't fulfill this need of romance before they committed to marriage. If it was good enough for you then, expecting them to come to your rescue after the fact is a difficult process. However, given the encouragement and proper direction, most men will rise to the cause if it means pleasing their wives in order to gain sexual pleasure. It is important their efforts be rewarded.

I live in a small town, one with a famous bed and breakfast inn. People come from far and wide to visit the Kintner House, and it is booked a great deal of the time. I love driving downtown and watching the "lovers" strolling around our quaint downtown square, especially on Friday nights. I can't help but smile when I see the interaction between the couple I'm observing at the moment. Inevitably, they're holding hands, walking leisurely, lost in time and each other. He is adoring her and giving in to her every desire. He stops in every small shop, window shops and buys her some souvenir to preserve the memory. He's stolen her away for the weekend, and she's all his. You can see the pride in his face. It's written all over him. He struts!

When I have the time, I love to return on Saturday morning and watch as the same couple exits the inn. His gait is more intensified. The affection is even more noticeable. It is obvious they have had a most enjoyable night. Their intimacy is heightened to degrees that will meld them and cause them to recall the history they created during this brief encounter for years to come.

A man will go to great lengths for a woman who strokes his ego, even occasionally. Most men are not nearly as needy in this area as are women. For the man, it typically takes only a small amount of effort to feed the ego, but the results are phenomenal.

Every man needs the assurance from his wife that he is providing in a manner satisfying her material needs. Being an adequate provider is of paramount importance to his self-esteem. If the family is suffering financially, it is extremely stressful to a man, and can be very damaging to his ego. Oftentimes, women can make a difference by being creative in cutting back in areas such as unnecessary food or clothing items. Upon close examination, there may be many nonessentials that could be pared away to ease the burden your husband may be feeling with regard to a financial crunch. Meeting the family budget is a secure place for your husband to be, and it is a huge relief of unnecessary stress for him, and your marriage.

We must also remember to guard our tongues in complaining about the lack of material possessions. Remember that anything you say with respect to what some neighbor down the street may have and you don't will be repeatedly played back in his head. Comments like these eventually trickle down into his heart and could, in turn, fracture a precious virtue of his. It's the very virtue we sometimes confuse to be a curse, but his ego is the driving force behind him. (Some men have more than their fair share.) It can either drive him to greatness or drive him into the ground. You are the shaft behind his drive.

MAKE PRAISE A HABIT

Praising *needs* to become habitual, but it must be *sincere*. Be observant of things, great and small, to be acknowledged and praised. Our unobservant nature may sow seeds of resentment and can result in the feeling of being taken for granted. Bear in mind all people and relationships are unique. This should become a way of life for you. Don't expect immediate results. If you praise once and, presto, great sex, what a special treat!

Praising your husband sets the mood in your home life, and the benefits of this positive reinforcement will spill over into the bedroom. Praise supplements his guarded male ego, and it has a calming effect. It settles one's soul and is a great sedative for the aggravations, hassles and worries of the day.

You will find that praising him for his performance in the bedroom will come easy, because he will perform remarkably well. Your pleasures will greatly increase as he strives to please you, thus enabling those praises to become even more sincere. Never forget the significance of complimenting his efforts in your intimate life. It is empowering to a man to know he has brought great pleasure to you sexually. Focus on the things he does right, and don't mention what he may have done wrong. If you didn't guide him while you were making love, it will serve no purpose to deflate him after you are finished. Preserve the intimacy by reflecting on what a great lover he is. When you have satisfied his deepest desires through recognizing and expressing his value and worth, you may rest in the assurance that he'll bring all his needs home to you.

11.

Protect Him

My wife has a slight impediment in her speech. Every now and then she stops to breathe.
JIMMY DURANTE

"HEY, LUCY, YOU'RE NEVER GONNA BELIEVE THIS!"

What is it about women that creates the need for us to share things with our friends? The I've-got-a-secret trait begins almost as soon as we begin to formulate sentences. When we were elementary age, we'd whisper to other little girls in the classroom. Once we hit puberty, we were chatting and telling everything under the sun about anyone we knew. By high school, there was not much sacred among friends. The college experience would mature us somewhat, but even by the time we were married, we found ourselves sharing a large part of our everyday lives with our friends.

We talk and talk and talk, and then wonder why men don't trust us. We give too much of ourselves away to others. We find ourselves confiding in our *best friends* today who may become our *distant friends* tomorrow, only to learn down the road that our friends broke the confidences we shared and the stories have become somewhat embellished. Most of us can identify with this scenario.

MUM'S THE WORD

Throughout our years in the ministry, my husband and I have encountered numerous couples who have been unable to reconcile their differences because one party, and typically the wife, has betrayed a confidence in the marriage. When the level of trust between husband and wife has been compromised, oftentimes it is impossible to recover from the damage that has been inflicted. We have also counseled couples who have been betrayed by one of the spouse's best friends because she/he shared a bit too much of confidential information about how well or how poorly a spouse performed in the bedroom. Consequently, the informed friend soon became the new lover to the friend's spouse.

By nature, men are private about their personal lives, and especially their performance in bed. It is enough for most male egos that they have satisfied their partner. When they fall short of this objective, they are rough enough on themselves without anyone pointing out what they perceive as a shortcoming. Boasting of our successes feels gratifying and positive. Pointing out failures only promotes a negative atmosphere at home, and it nestles in for a long winter's nap in your bed.

We must protect our husbands. They are the ones who have promised to love and cherish us. If your husband is a man who is honoring God in his life, it is important to him that you respect the way he accomplishes this. We know all of his faults and weaknesses. And you know what? So does he. The beauty of teamwork is for you to be his strength in areas where he falls short and to find cause to praise his attributes rather than constantly point out his faults. He looks to you to be his support through good times and the not-so-good times.

When we fall out with our husbands, it really should be the business of no one else. Many differences between spouses are ironed-out before the sun goes down. If you have shared with Betty the dispute you had this morning with Tim, she will probably still be dwelling on it tomorrow, and who knows who else she will have told in between. You and Tim are over your spat, but Betty thinks he's a rat!

I would strongly encourage you to give your disputes time to work themselves out. They usually are put to rest within a short amount of time if you openly communicate with each other. This aspect of confidentiality in marriage is an area that should be brought into accord by the husband and wife or, should the situation be dire,

Never discuss your husband's faults with your friends.

a third party of their mutual choice. Again, I would emphasize that not all men are amenable to working on problems within the marriage. In earlier chapters, I have addressed the importance of not feeling like a failure personally if your husband does not love and honor you as Christ has instructed.

This is a powerful standard to apply within your marriage: ***never discuss your husband's faults with your friends***. It is demeaning, degrading, and quite disrespectful. It is very humiliating and a tremendous ego-deflater should he learn he has been the brunt of the daily pipeline. When this sort of behavior becomes a part of your routine, it can quickly bring about the demise of your marriage. You can begin to lose confidence in your husband and to focus only on his faults. If he realizes you have divulged what you perceive as a flaw in his character, he is most likely to become very despondent and unwilling to make an effort to correct the problem.

While everyday issues of ins-and-outs might be recoverable in a troubled marriage, I can assure you, if you betray your intimate, private life to an outsider, it will greatly impede any chance of reconciliation. And let me hasten to add, this sort of behavior can shake the very foundation of a solid marriage. Breaking the confidence of your bedroom manner is an absolute taboo of a marital relationship. It can be more damaging than the comparison issue I addressed earlier.

WAGGING TONGUE

I can recall very early in our marriage, and our ministry, attending a ladies' retreat. There were approximately twenty ladies in one cabin with bunk-beds when the discussion of some of the women's husbands' performances in the bedroom became the topic of conversation. I was amazed at the number of women who were critical about their intimate activities with their spouses. News spread quickly about the night's conversation, and many men were tainted from that moment. I have come to witness the eventual dissolution of several marriages of these women who spoke unfavorably about their intimacy with their husbands. Don't ever believe what you say in a women's group is completely confidential. It is a rarity if you have experienced this phenomenon of nature!

BETRAYAL

I was consoling Ginny, a beautiful young lady who was sharing with me the mistakes she felt she had made in her failed marriage. She was lamenting how she wished she had listened to me when I warned her not to talk about her husband's faults to anyone. We had talked on several occasions, and I had cautioned her of the dangers lurking if she shared her problems in the marriage with others. Women are trusting people by nature. We honestly believe when we tell one of our friends something in strictest confidence, it will fall on no other ears. My heart broke for Ginny as I sat and listened to her story unfold.

While she realized the fault was not entirely hers, she was intuitively aware she had not protected her ex-husband's privacy as she should have. Ginny had confided in her best friend Deborah about her troubled marriage. She had told Deborah about things her spouse had encouraged her to do such as losing weight, becoming active in sports, to initiate sex more, and numerous other confidences that Ginny soon realized she should have kept to herself. Deborah set her sights on Ginny's Tom. She used all of Ginny's confidences in the betrayal. She became involved in the sports activities Tom was involved in. She worked out with him at the gym. One can be quite certain Deborah made sexual advances that lured him into her trap. She capitalized on Ginny's restless marriage. With friends like Deborah, who needs a husband anyway? Good thing, because he was gone.

Ginny is more cautious about her personal matters today. She understands that should she find love again and be involved in a marital setting, she will keep the business of the marriage to herself. Twice burned, a lesson learned. Double betrayal seems to sting the most.

LOVE SPEAKS A THOUSAND WORDS

Outward expressions of affection and respect between couples speak volumes regarding their intimate lives. When husbands and wives regard each other with dignity and respect, their bedroom manner leaves no room for criticism. My husband and I are often asked if we are newlyweds! After many years of marriage, it is gratifying to know we still present ourselves as fresh and vibrant lovers. We have managed to preserve the intimacy in our marriage.

If you must say anything about your husband's performance in bed, speak of what a great lover he is. If it gets back to him that he's Tarzan or Superman in bed, he'll be able to handle that. Anything short of grand and glorious will absolutely crush his ego. This is a very serious matter to your husband and should be treated with the utmost delicacy, confidentiality, trust, and absolute privacy.

> *When husbands and wives regard each other with dignity and respect, their bedroom manner leaves no room for criticism.*

12.
Pray with Him

"For where two or three come together in my name, there am I with them."

(JESUS, MATT. 18:20 NIV)

Briefly I will explore with you the benefits of praying with your spouse. I find it very interesting how few Christian couples pray together—*together* being the key word here. It is as difficult for some couples to pray together as it is for them to openly discuss sex. I find that truly odd. You sleep with this person, you bare your soul, this person sees your nakedness, knows when you blunder, when you stumble, when you hurt, when you're happy and when you're sad. Yet, you find it difficult to pray with him?

Oftentimes the women are very willing; it is the men who struggle in this area. Men are called to be the leaders in the home, but find it difficult to pray with their wives. If this is your situation, what can you do to overcome this stumbling block in your relationship? As the manager of the home, be creative in your attempts to make him feel more comfortable in the setting of prayer time with you and the family.

MEALTIME IS A GREAT START

Start with mealtime prayer. We taught our kids to pray for specifics. Many times, because of our hectic schedules, our evening meal was the only opportunity we had to pray together as a family. Everyone had to pray something. Now our daughters and their husbands have incorporated this exercise into their family mealtimes. Even your more timid family personalities kick in with practice. They soon find many things to pray about.

The women who have taken this advice have reported good things. It's hard to resist, "Daddy, your turn." Daddy will usually, while not always, step up and find something to pray about. It's simplistic conversation with God. Needs and concerns are brought before Him, and it's exciting to everyone when they witness answered prayers. So, start simple, and mealtime is a great beginning to introduce a husband-wife prayer life.

COUPLE PRAYER TIME

Just do it. Take the plunge. Pray privately with your spouse. If he does not wish to take the lead and pray, ask him if he will join you as *you* pray. Hold hands and *you* pray for the two of you. Eventually, most men will come around and join you in prayer. Become even bolder with him and get down on your knees together. There is a humbling quality associated with the act of kneeling before God in unison. It is an act that will equalize you, yet hold your husband out as a real leader within your marriage. He doesn't have to define it for you; you will sense the power of guidance to which he aspires after revealing his heart to the Heavenly Father. The two of you will begin to compose a depth in your spiritual lives that will provide a fortress against the most contemptible forces.

It is as difficult for some couples to pray together as it is for them to openly discuss sex.

There will be some season in your lives as a married couple that will call for fervent prayer. Use the opportunity to encourage this dynamic premise in your marriage. If your husband has not joined you in combined prayer, his spirit may be open to surrendering to this strong principle. I know there are, as always, exceptions to every rule; that's a given. Don't ever give up. You keep praying anyway.

Prayer is the telescope to your spouse's heart. It is a transparency of emotions he may not allow you to see otherwise. When he begins to join you in prayer, you will begin to learn a wealth of information about the support he needs from you. Some men never share all that may be going on at work, but in their prayer life you may catch a

Prayer is the telescope to your spouse's heart.

glimmer of an unsettling situation. Learn to read between the lines (we always expect him to) so that you will know when his heart is especially burdened over something.

Here again, you will reap the rewards of this. He will be able to see inside your heart and begin to understand what may be troubling you. It is a valuable tool to facilitate conversation between the two of you, even though it is conversation with God. Many times it will be the only chance you get to communicate earnestly with each other in a day's time.

You will pray for things you both have an investment in: children, jobs, family members, friends, and church. The investment is priceless; the prayer bonding. Praying together takes on a different flavor and tone than any single act you do together as a couple. Issues that may be tense between you, when brought up in prayer, seem to be less stressful. Your plea for certain situations to be resolved is more tender and considerate. You wield yourself into a different posture when you're before the Lord in prayer. It brings your life as a couple into harmonic balance and extraordinary calmness. It is a powerful way to begin your day when you have corporately praised the Lord and brought your children, each other, and all your burdens before God's throne.

OFFER YOUR MARRIAGE TO GOD

Whether you pray alone or with your husband, offer your marriage to the Lord for blessing. He doesn't want to see something He has ordained fail. He will do what you allow Him to do to keep it together. You must be willing parties to make it possible for Him to work in your lives. Keeping your marriage finely tuned takes teamwork. Don't exclude God from your team. While keeping your focus on Him does not give you full immunity to difficulties, you will be able to move mountains at the call of His name.

Offer your marriage to the Lord for blessing.

Aspire to keep your marriage in a beautiful place. You have gone through the tips. They have been proven to strengthen and secure your marriage. Spending time in prayer with respect to the execution of these values will aid you in each aspect. Reassuring God of your commitment to your marriage will solidify your heart's intentions every day. Seeking guidance from Him with regard to the shaping of your attitude will find you gifting to yourself an enormous amount of self-control. Naturally, the self-control will spill over into your decision to get in shape and be attractive for him. When you feel beautiful, it is energizing. Feeling pretty about yourself motivates you to prepare your bed, to playfully flirt, and, ultimately, to perform and bring exquisite sexual satisfaction for both of you. Your prayer will bolster you into a level of comfort in communicating your needs and training him in

A happy home means you protect its history for generations to come.

an area that he'll be more than willing to be coached through. Attaining the level of intimacy that God intended for you to enjoy in your marriage will launch you into a pattern of praising him, not just in the bedroom but publicly, as well, about all facets of your lives together. You will find yourself protecting him from not only your tongue but also anyone else who takes a jab at him. Woe unto the person who puts down your man!

Your prayer life relating specifically to your intimacy with your husband will snowball into a balance of magical romance. Not every day will either of you feel the Cinderella/Prince Charming high, so don't set your expectations beyond reach. But, your night out to the Ball will come around more often for you. Once you savor the flavor of first-time romance again with your husband, you will have an unquenchable thirst for your special moments.

Ask the Lord to write on your heart the wisdom to discern your husband's needs. God will give you an astute recognition of your man's desires. And while you're at it, ask Him to help you manage your time in order to accomplish this. *You have not because you ask not.* Prayerfully, your husband will be willing to sit and pray with you. Revealing your heart's desires to the Lord will soften your husband's heart and make him receptive to your consuming desire to preserve the intimacy of your marriage. God understands that the preservation of this wonderful gift synchronizes all other areas of your home life. A happy home means you protect its history for generations to come. What better model for relationships than one fashioned through prayer.

13.
The Dark Season

With all due fear, honor and respect of the Lord, I have come to realize that His Holy breathed, inspired Scripture may contain one misinterpretation. It is found in Genesis 3:16 where God punishes Eve for eating of the forbidden fruit and proclaims her pains of childbirth will greatly increase. I'm quite certain God, in His infinite wisdom, was well aware man would come to discover ways to circumvent pain for women. My husband cringes each time I suggest to him that perhaps Moses misunderstood the Lord and truly meant to write not only would her pain in childbirth increase, but that she would come to know the *dark season* in her life and be stripped of life as she had come to love it in her younger years on earth!

I'm equally convinced God would have never named the menstrual cycle our "friend." Not many of us enjoy friends who bring such pain. And for those of you who have not yet experienced the graduated version of "your friend," prepare yourselves for the biggest betrayal of friendship you'll ever come to know. Truly menopause was the ultimate punishment Eve would bear. And all the menopausal women said? Amen!

Many physicians feel menopause may be brought on full force by some significant stressor(s) in a woman's life. If this is, indeed, the case, mine would have been the death of my mother. Due to some extreme circumstances surrounding her medical care, she began an eight-week nightmare of her death. Once the family decided it was time to release her from life support, the ensuing thirty-two hours and five minutes would prove to be an experience for which no one is ever prepared. Of the eight siblings in the family, it fell to me to walk her to Heaven's gate. I'm certain that God granted me the strength to take on the task, and I am grateful I was able to do this for my siblings. None of them should have witnessed the image of our mother drawing her last breath in the manner it presented itself due to an unprofessional medical situation.

I felt an immediate process of change within my body. I realized the tremendous stress I had undergone during this time period was life-altering for me. Emotionally, the loss of a parent carries with it its share of burdens. Physically, I had undergone some sort of transformation. I would come to realize all too soon that along with my mother, my *youth* had died as well. Within the year after her death, I would embrace the horrors of, you got it, menopause!

HORNS—A DEAD GIVE-AWAY!

I thought I might be in trouble when it appeared I grew horns and my claws assumed an always-alert-and-ready-for-war position. The hot flashes and night sweats began to set in. It was becoming increasingly apparent I might have a real problem going on inside my physical body when I could visualize myself stripping off my clothes and lying in the middle of the conference room table while I was taking depositions. No matter how hot I got, however, never would you see me fan! I decided years ago, when I began to take notice of my more mature friends approaching the change of life, that I would not succumb to ever wearing the designer label of "Menopausal, by God" on my sleeve. I began to worry about my frame of mind, however, when I considered masquerading as a refrigerator to a Halloween party. Considering this to be a dead give-away to my menopausal condition, I quickly dismissed the idea. Never let 'em see you sweat!

Ignoring the issue held this dreaded disorder at bay for a few months. The sleep deprivation that had invaded my nights was finding me devoid of the usual energy and enthusiasm to which I had always been accustomed. Being a person who can perform on very little sleep (you learn to function on minimum rest when you grow up on a farm), I was able to carry through my days on two hours of sleep with little attention to my mayhem.

At some point during this term of torture, I began gaining weight by merely breathing. I had not quite figured out in my head how I was going to turn off the oxygen in order to lose weight. I increased my workout time at the gymnasium from one hour to two hours, and longer when time permitted. I cut down my caloric intake to 1200 calories a day, give or take a few. With the 500 to 600 calories I was burning at the gym, I was hoping to offset the extra weight that seemed to continue rapidly creeping up and holding prayer meeting around my hips and thighs. I contemplated stapling my lips shut at times when my appetite seemed exceedingly ravenous. The weight gain was a particularly disturbing part of this process for me. I began to feel I was getting close to a breaking point emotionally with this new-fangled season in my life.

I strongly considered offering my body for scientific research. After all, I was certain some alien form had found a host inside me. I was becoming someone no one recognized. My mirror was reflecting inspection labels of "Rejected" when I would stand before it naked! My concerns deepened the first time I locked myself in the bathroom to take a shower. My husband, unaccustomed to this new behavior of mine, was dumbfounded when he attempted to get in to brush his teeth before leaving for work. It was totally unlike me to *hide away* and adopt this new state of modesty. When I finally relinquished the bathroom that morning, it was awfully sweet and comforting when he came up to me, tenderly embraced me and said, "Lil' Buddy (that's his endearing term for me), we're in this together. Everything's gonna be all right. You'll always be my beautiful lady." Aaah. What a man!

TAKING CHARGE

While his words settled this beast that had set up camp inside me, there were still times my family and friends were certain some unexplained life-form might devour them without due warning. It would take little to nothing to set it off, and I'd find myself in a tailspin once again. This was not going to be a pleasant journey, and the best I could hope for was it would soon give way to exhaustion as I refused to alter my busy lifestyle. (I would later learn my hormonal imbalance had disrupted my thyroid levels, as happens in many cases.)

It was not until I realized my sex drive was diminishing that I decided it was time to address this problem once and for all. That was the final straw! I was convinced more than ever about my theory of the misinterpreted scripture.

I still believe today had I really put it to the test, my unwavering preacher husband could have been convinced as well! This was serious business. It's one thing to mess with me, but now you're messing with him, too. All right, that does it. This is war. You want a fight, *Mr. Meno Pause*, you got it! The battle was on.

I read everything on menopause I could get my hands on within the month. I had made the decision years ago I never wanted to be put on generic hormones. I am definitely one of a kind, and since I'm not cut of the same mold as every Janie, Jeanie and Judy, I would go to my grave without ever ingesting a common drug designed for one class of women, i.e., all of them!

I had prepared myself when I turned fifty for the upcoming onslaught of menopause. I attended all-day wellness clinics held in nearby cities and began digesting alternative solutions for the time when I would need to make my decision. A soy-based bioidentical hormone therapy had seemed to be the path for me. I would

> *You want a fight,* Mr. Meno Pause, *you got it!*

neatly tuck the materials and business cards away and make plans to retrieve the knowledge I had gained when necessary. It had now become necessary.

The Lord and I have a discussion about this every morning. I'm so glad He has a sense of humor. I'm quite certain He has selective hearing. He knew husbands would need that quality; that's why He made them in His own image! God, just like my husband, ignores my ranting and raving about the extra pounds, the new wardrobe I need, and the total disgust at this new darkness that has befallen me. This too shall pass, and all three of us will be happy when it does.

NINETY-THREE, AND SHE'S STILL HUMMIN'

It is interesting, this perpetual desire women possess for their maintenance of sexuality. If you recall, the third principle set forth in this book, "The Look," reflects the flirtatious, prissy little miss at a tender age froo-frooing and taking care to make herself presentable. This aspect of our makeup is no less important in our menopausal years than it is when we're two. It is an element in us that God intended to be venerated, not only in our eyes, but in the eyes of the beholder.

Being wanted, needed and desired is essential in whatever season a woman finds herself.

I always enjoy shopping at the grocery stores and running into one of our more *mature* ladies dressed to the nines with her makeup, purse and gloves, her nicest flat heels, and all accessories in place. It is a precious sight to behold. It exemplifies such grace and charm, sandwiched in between such resolve and determination to hold onto the one thing no one can take from her without her permission – her sexuality.

It is natural that we, as women, take pride in how we present ourselves to our world, no matter the size of that space. It is vital to our well-being for us to maintain a healthy opinion about our feminine qualities and their value to our partner. Being wanted, needed and desired is essential in whatever season a woman finds herself. From her youngest, most tender, youthful years to her wiser, more weathered, experienced ones, this one ingredient continues to flavor her life.

EVER ON GUARD

Menopause does its very best to rob you of your most prized possession. Be ever so careful and on constant guard during this season in your life. Your husband's needs go on. Few women will share their hearts about this sensitive subject. It can be a demeaning, disgraceful, and heart-wrenching time in your life. It is difficult to struggle with losing such an important part of yourself. Your loss is one that can strip you of your womanhood. It can make you feel less vital in every walk of life. Be careful not to allow such thoughts to filter through your psyche and rob you of your significance to everyone around you. You are still very much the beautiful person God created you to be. You are a vital part of your family and friends, and someone who can't afford to get lost in the depression menopause can lead to.

If you're not careful to guard your heart, you can feel out of control of very important issues. Intimacy with your husband is one issue many times overlooked. I feel very fortunate to have an understanding mate. Many of my friends have not been so fortunate. Be cautious not to allow your season of darkness to become an invitation for your husband to engage in a mid-life crisis. I have known many men to do this of their own volition, but you do not want to feel as though you have contributed to this betrayal in your relationship. He will need you to address his sexual desires even though there will be times you will be absolutely devoid of the desire yourself. It is easy to use your convenient *new-found friend* as an excuse to retire for the evening without satisfying him sexually. This is a time when you will need to adjust your attitude to that of *Honey, you are more important than I am.* A truly devoted man of God will have a tender heart about this strange new development that has surfaced in you. The two of you will come through your **dark** season still deeply in love.

Be cautious not to allow your season of darkness to become an invitation for your husband to engage in a mid-life crisis.

Conclusion

There isn't time—so brief is life—for bickering, apologies, heartburnings, callings to account. There is only time for loving & but an instant, so to speak, for that.

MARK TWAIN
LETTER TO CLARA SPAULDING
8/20/1886

There is no greater priority for a couple than preserving the intimacy of marriage. As this book has unfolded, I pray you will have begun to understand the elements it takes to attain a fulfilled marital relationship. If you and your partner have found your marriage to be just a bit ho-hum, it is reparable. These tips for pleasing your husband are a great beginning for you. They are realistic and within your reach. Women oftentimes are the initiators of innovation and change in many areas within the family unit. We can be in this arena, also, only to learn making love will be more gratifying than we ever dreamed possible.

Make your sexual equation complete. Each of these steps builds on the other. Being committed, having a great attitude, acquiring the look, preparing the bed, playing with him, performing with and for him, training him, praising him, protecting him, and praying with him, all add up to God's perfect plan for the preservation of the holy state of matrimony.

Works Cited

"Christians Are More Likely to Experience Divorce Than Are Non-Christians." Barna Research Group. *http://www.barna.org/cgi-bin/*. Dec. 21, 1999. Accessed Sep. 22, 2005.

"Directory of Mark Twain's Maxims, Quotations, and Various Opinions." *www.twainquotes.com.* Accessed May 22, 2002.

Estes, Richard, Ph.D. and Weiner, Neil, Ph.D. "The Commercial Sexual Exploitation of Children in the U.S., Canada and Mexico." *restes@ssw.upenn.edu.* Sep. 10, 2001. Accessed Sep. 22, 2005.

Fisher, Helen. *Why We Love: The Nature and Chemistry of Romantic Love.* Owl Books. Jan. 2, 2005.

Elle Magazine, "Good Sex With a Not So Good Lover," Jan. 2006.

Fox News. Transcript. "Gary Haugen on Tsunami Children at Risk." Jan. 2005. *http://www.foxnews.com/printer_friendly_story/0,3566,143643,00.html.* Accessed July 2005.

Gray, John, Ph.D. *Men Are from Mars, Women Are from Venus: A Practical Guide for Improving Communications and Getting What You Want in Your Relationships.* HarperCollins Publishers; 1st edition (May, 1992).

Haugen, Gary. "Freeing Captives of the International Sex Trade." The 700 Club. Jan. 2005. CBN.com. The Christian Broadcasting Network. *http://www.cbn.com/ 700club/guests/bios/gary_haugen_010705.html.* Accessed March 2005.

Monroe, Valerie. "Sex is Sublime." *O The Oprah Magazine.* Oct. 2004, pp. 264-68.

Phillips, Nancy, M.D. "Female Sexual Dysfunction: Evaluation and Treatment." *www.aafp.org.* July 1, 2000. Accessed Sep. 22, 2005.

"Teen Pregnancy Statistics." 2005 About, Inc., A part of the New York Times Company.

"2003 Statistical Abstract of the U.S." Table 83 on p. 4 of pdf of Section 2. *http://www.census.gov/prod/2004pubs/ 03statab/vitstat.pdf.* Accessed 2005.